WELCOME TO AMAZING HISTORY

The world as we know it has been shaped by the past. Tools have evolved over thousands of years; species have thrived then died out; civilisations have risen and fallen. Now it's time to uncover what came before us.

In Amazing History, meet the animals that ruled the roost in the prehistoric period, and find your way through the ancient Egyptian underworld. Spend some time at the Tower of London – just try not to get yourself executed – and learn how to make the best sword before discovering how warfare changed in the 20th century with the advent of the Royal Air Force and the development of the tank. But our history isn't limited to Earth; take a trip to space as you learn about the launch of NASA over 60 years ago.

With all this and more waiting to be revealed, it's time to turn the page and find out how we got to be where we are today.

FUTURE

AMAZING HISTORY

Future PLC Quay House, The Ambury, Bath, BA1 1UA

Editorial
Editor **Katharine Marsh**
Designer **Katy Stokes**
Compiled by **Charles Ginger & Eva Garis**
Senior Art Editor **Andy Downes**
Head of Art & Design **Greg Whitaker**
Editorial Director **Jon White**

Cover images
Joe Cummings & Getty Images

Photography
All copyrights and trademarks are recognised and respected

Advertising
Media packs are available on request
Commercial Director **Clare Dove**

International
Head of Print Licensing **Rachel Shaw**
licensing@futurenet.com
www.futurecontenthub.com

Circulation
Head of Newstrade **Tim Mathers**

Production
Head of Production **Mark Constance**
Production Project Manager **Matthew Eglinton**
Advertising Production Manager **Joanne Crosby**
Digital Editions Controller **Jason Hudson**
Production Managers **Keely Miller, Nola Cokely,
Vivienne Calvert, Fran Twentyman**

Printed in the UK

Distributed by Marketforce, 5 Churchill Place, Canary Wharf, London, E14 5HU
www.marketforce.co.uk Tel: 0203 787 9001

How It Works Amazing History Third Edition (HIB4624)
© 2022 Future Publishing Limited

We are committed to only using magazine paper which is derived from responsibly managed,
certified forestry and chlorine-free manufacture. The paper in this bookazine was sourced
and produced from sustainable managed forests, conforming to strict environmental and
socioeconomic standards.

All contents © 2022 Future Publishing Limited or published under licence. All rights reserved.
No part of this magazine may be used, stored, transmitted or reproduced in any way without
the prior written permission of the publisher. Future Publishing Limited (company number
2008885) is registered in England and Wales. Registered office: Quay House, The Ambury,
Bath BA1 1UA. All information contained in this publication is for information only and is, as far
as we are aware, correct at the time of going to press. Future cannot accept any responsibility
for errors or inaccuracies in such information. You are advised to contact manufacturers and
retailers directly with regard to the price of products/services referred to in this publication. Apps
and websites mentioned in this publication are not under our control. We are not responsible for
their contents or any other changes or updates to them. This magazine is fully independent and
not affiliated in any way with the companies mentioned herein.

FUTURE Connectors.
Creators.
Experience
Makers.

Future plc is a public
company quoted on the
London Stock Exchange
(symbol: FUTR)
www.futureplc.com

Chief executive **Zillah Byng-Thorne**
Non-executive chairman **Richard Huntingford**
Chief Financial and Strategy Officer **Penny Ladkin-Brand**

Tel +44 (0)1225 442 244

Part of the

HOW IT WORKS

bookazine series

Widely
Recycled

ipso. For press freedom
with responsibility

CONTENTS

EVERYTHING YOU NEED TO KNOW ABOUT THE WORLD WE LIVED IN

8

22

32

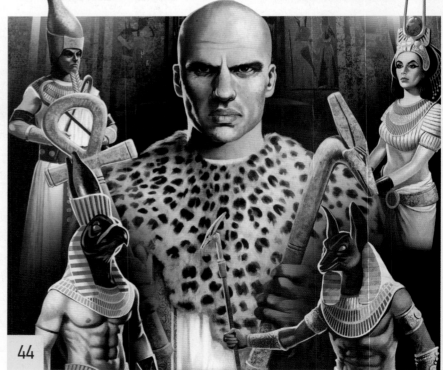

44

54

64

76

86

102

MODERN HISTORY

THE 20TH CENTURY

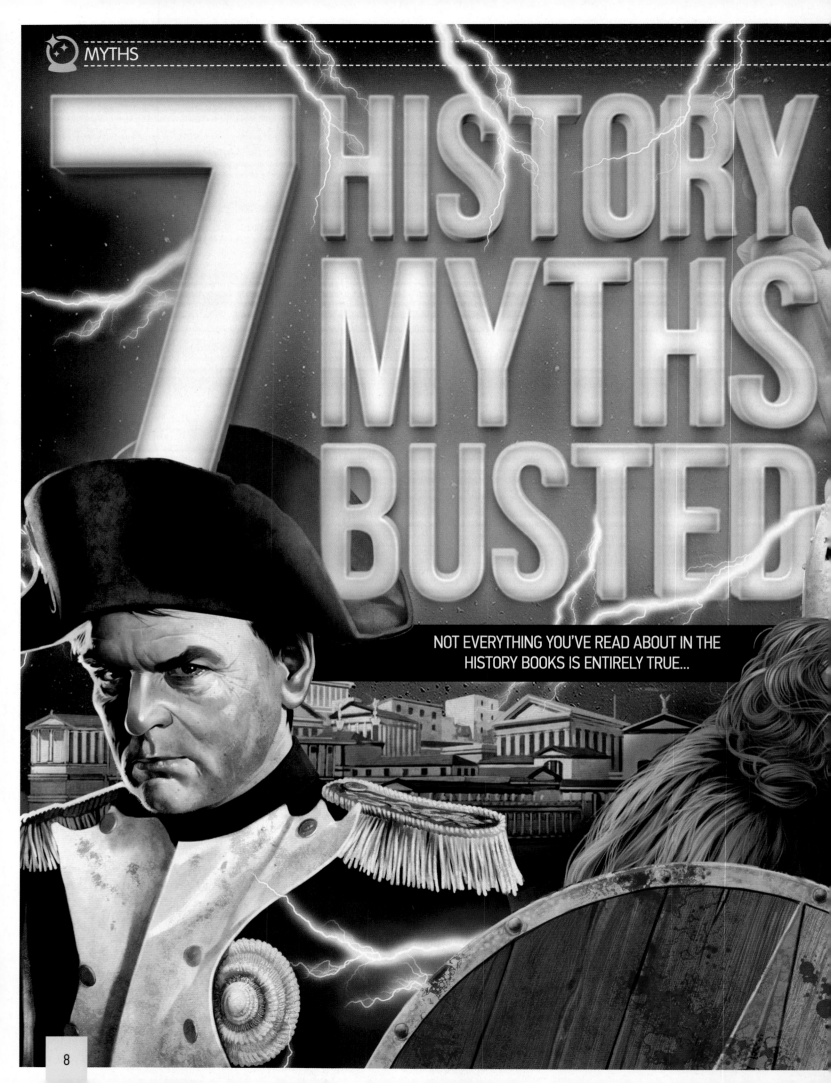

7 HISTORY MYTHS BUSTED

NOT EVERYTHING YOU'VE READ ABOUT IN THE HISTORY BOOKS IS ENTIRELY TRUE...

BELOW
Armour grew progressively thicker in later centuries to protect against the threat of firearms

Image Source • Joe Cummings

1 "KNIGHTS HAD TO BE HOISTED ONTO THEIR HORSES"

Although they look incredibly heavy, 15th-century suits of armour weigh in at around 14-23 kilograms (31-50 pounds). Despite this, they were not difficult to move about in or mount a horse while wearing. Knights had to remain as agile as possible in order to stay combat-effective, or even just survive a melee. If armour really had been so heavy that a fallen knight could not have stood up again on his own, or been able to re-mount his horse, the smallest trip in battle would have been a death sentence.

While the metal plates had to be tough enough for ample protection, they also had to be light enough for prolonged action and at least some range of movement. As such, a suit of plate

armour could be comprised of around 18 main separate pieces, each protecting a different limb or vital organ. Importantly, each piece had to move flexibly with the wearer, and without restricting any movement like a sword swing or even some light running.

One of the origins of the impossibly heavy armour is found in the 1944 film *Henry V*, an adaptation of the play by William Shakespeare, produced by Laurence Olivier. This depicts knights being hoisted onto their mounts using cranes – a bizarre fiction with absolutely no historical evidence. By contrast, there are accounts of armoured soldiers performing almost acrobatic feats, including French fighter

Bertrand du Guesclin, who made his name during the Hundred Years' War, who is recorded leaping to and from his horse.

Modern-day soldiers, by comparison, regularly take more than 50 kilograms (110 pounds) of armour, weaponry and equipment into combat, the majority of which is carried in their backpacks. With a suit of armour, the weight is spread mostly evenly over the wearer's entire body, making it much easier to bear and balance while wearing. This means that far from being restricted by impossibly heavy armour, knights fighting centuries ago were arguably more light and agile than their 21st-century counterparts.

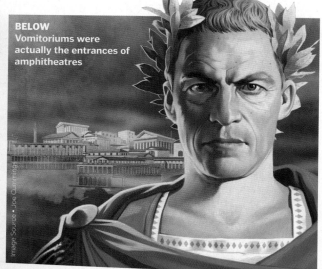

BELOW
Vomitoriums were actually the entrances of amphitheatres

2 "ANNE BOLEYN HAD AN EXTRA FINGER"

Famous for being the doomed second wife of the notorious Henry VIII, Anne Boleyn was hit with charges of adultery, incest and high treason. She had faced many accusations, especially towards the end of her life, but having an extra finger wasn't one of them. In fact, the claim wasn't even made during her lifetime.

Decades after Boleyn's death, a Catholic propagandist called Nicholas Sander wrote that she had "a projecting tooth under the upper lip, and on her right hand, six fingers". He added that she had a large wart under her chin.

In Tudor England physical imperfections were thought to be a sign of evil, and Sander had portrayed Boleyn as a witch who had seduced the king. But would such an unsightly woman have captured the heart of the Tudor tyrant? It seems very unlikely, for so determined was Henry to marry her that he broke away from the Roman Catholic Church and established his own – the Church of England.

Nicholas Sander never actually met Boleyn in person and was only a boy when she was beheaded in 1536. It's likely that Anne's rumoured disfigurements were a way of discrediting her daughter, Queen Elizabeth I. It was her religious policies that forced Sander into exile, and he wasn't alone in attacking the Protestant monarch's parentage in a vengeful bid to sully her name.

What's more, Anne's first biographer, George Wyatt, had spoken to those who knew her and admitted that while she did have several moles and an extra nail on her little finger, there was no sixth digit. And when a body believed to have been Boleyn was exhumed at the Tower of London in the 19th century, there was no evidence to support Sander's slander.

3 "VOMITORIUMS WERE USED FOR THROWING UP IN"

The Romans were fond of a feast, and they would gorge on delicacies like wild boar, pheasant, lobsters and songbirds until they couldn't eat any more. That's when they would take a trip to the vomitorium – a room where the diner could expel their previous courses and then return to eat some more. Or so pop culture would have us believe.

In ancient Rome, vomitoriums were actually the entrance and exit passages of amphitheatres. The 5th-century writer Macrobius chose this charming Latin word because of the way people "spewed forth" into their seats at these open-air venues.

It seems people may have got confused over time, which isn't surprising given the infamous gluttony of some of Rome's rulers. Claudius was said to always finish a meal bloated and confined to bed, while Vitellius allegedly ate the sacrificial meat from an altar! But even the mighty emperors didn't have a special chunder chamber.

Image Source • Joe Cummings

Image Source • James Gillray

BELOW
This cartoon of Napoleon by artist James Gillray shows the 'little' emperor ranting and raving at the freedoms in England

4 "NAPOLEON WAS SHORT"

Despite conquering much of Europe single-handedly, Napoleon Bonaparte is almost as well known for his short stature. But in reality, the emperor of France was around 1.69 metres (five feet, 6.5 inches) tall, making him above average height for men in both France and England at that time.

When he died in 1821, Napoleon was measured to be 1.57 metres (five foot, two inches) tall. Unfortunately for the deceased, this was taken in French feet and inches, which were slightly larger than English measurements. In the early 19th century the metric system was not yet used universally, meaning there was no standarised measurement. When interpreted as English feet, Napoleon's height was therefore mistakenly recorded as being over four inches shorter.

However, even before his death the emperor had been mocked for his supposed tiny size. Another source of this myth is found in the British press of the period. Newspaper columns roundly criticised Napoleon, printing caricatures depicting him as a tiny child throwing temper tantrums. This impression was aided by his nickname 'Le Petit Caporal' (the little corporal) among his troops, and the fact his personal bodyguard, the Old Guard, had a minimum height requirement of 1.8 metres (six feet), and so they towered above him by comparison.

This myth has proven so persuasive that a theoretical condition was named after the emperor's supposedly short stature. The 'Napoleon complex' suggests that shorter-than-average men become more aggressive, seek more attention in social gatherings and possess greater ambition than average-height or tall men. Experts still question the accuracy of this, but what's certain is that Napoleon was by no means vertically challenged.

5 "300 SPARTANS ALONE FOUGHT THE PERSIAN ARMY AT THERMOPYLAE"

In 480 BCE, King Leonidas made a brave last stand against a horde of enemies at the head of only 300 of his ferocious hoplite warriors. It is one of the most compelling stories of ancient Greece, but is it entirely true?

In reality, between 6,000 and 7,000 fellow Greeks joined the Spartans at the Battle of Thermopylae, travelling from across Greece to defend against the Persian invasion led by King Xerxes I. Among those fighting with the 300 Spartans, Herodotus lists 700 Thespians, 400 Thebans, 1,120 Arcadians, 1,000 Phocians, and more. Nonetheless, the Greeks were still greatly outnumbered against up to 100,000 Persian soldiers.

The Greek army was deployed in a narrow coastal pass, nicknamed the Hot Gate, where the overwhelming numbers of attacking Persians could not be effected. According to Herodotus, the crucial turning point in the battle came when the Persian army was led to a secret mountain pass, enabling them to overcome the Phocian guards.

In the 2006 film *300*, it is at this point that the Spartans' allies abandon them out of fear, while Leonidas declares he and his men will stay and fight to the death. However, even this scene is inaccurate, as several of the Greek allies remained fighting to the bitter end, including those forces from Thespiae and Thebes.

While the Thespians reportedly stayed willingly with Leonidas, Herodotus writes that the king kept the Theban troops against their will. Regardless, the Persian army eventually crushed their Greek opponents, who had fought their way into legend.

Image Source • Joe Cummings

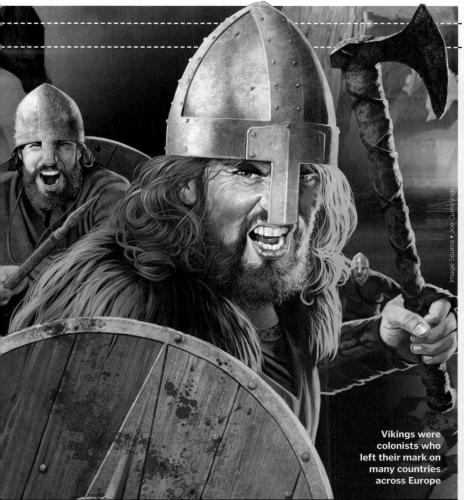

Vikings were colonists who left their mark on many countries across Europe

7 "MARIE ANTOINETTE SAID 'LET THEM EAT CAKE'"

When the wife of King Louis XVI was told her French subjects had no bread to eat, she retorted, "Let them eat cake." Or did she? It was 1789, crop failures had left the starving population deeply resentful of the monarchy, and the Austrian-born queen became their target. However, the phrase 'let them eat cake' had been used for years. More than a century earlier, Marie-Thérèse – the Spanish bride of King Louis XIV – supposedly said the French people should eat "the crust of the pâté".

The infamous remark stuck though, and Marie Antoinette's reputation for decadence was blamed for causing the country's economic downturn. While it's true that she embraced life at Versailles, her love of palace parties, fashion and gambling wasn't the cause of the French Revolution. Nevertheless, the misunderstood monarch was sentenced to death along with the rest of the royal family, but the myth survived her.

6 "VIKINGS WORE HORNED HELMETS"

Vikings were seafaring Scandinavians that raided, traded and garnered a bloodthirsty reputation between the 8th and 11th centuries. The famous beastly horned helmets seem to fit the stereotype, but there's actually no evidence to suggest they ever wore them.

This myth was popularised after writers and artists used the headgear in their portrayals of Vikings. In the 1870s, German costume designer Carl Emil Doepler created horned helmets for Wagner's Norse-inspired opera, and so he is often credited with cementing this stereotype. Perhaps these creators were inspired by 19th-century archaeological discoveries of horned helmets – but these were later found to predate the Vikings.

The only shred of evidence that can be called 'Viking' was discovered at a Gjermundbu burial mound, but this 10th-century artifact does not have any horns. It's possible such helmets were used for ceremonial purposes, but it's very unlikely they were worn aboard warships – the space would have been too limited – and they wouldn't be practical in battle either. Instead, it's thought that Norsemen wore leather skullcaps or domed metal helmets with brow ridges, fragments of which have been discovered. It could also be possible that some Vikings didn't wear any headgear at all, which would explain why only a small number of helmets have been found.

That's not the only myth surrounding the Vikings, though. Portrayed as beardy, illiterate savages, we've since discovered they groomed themselves with combs and razors; they developed a complex alphabet of runes; and while some spilled a lot of blood in their bid to conquer foreign lands, others earned a peaceful living through farming and trading.

BELOW
Marie Antoinette being led to her execution on 16 October 1793

PREHISTORY

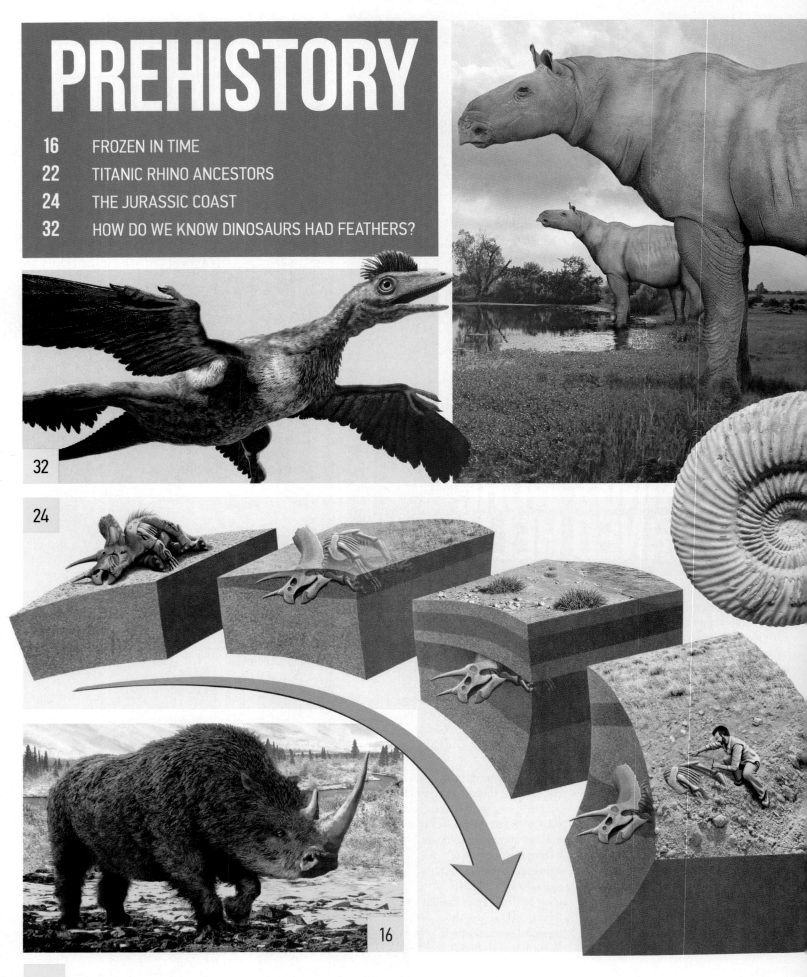

32

24

16

14

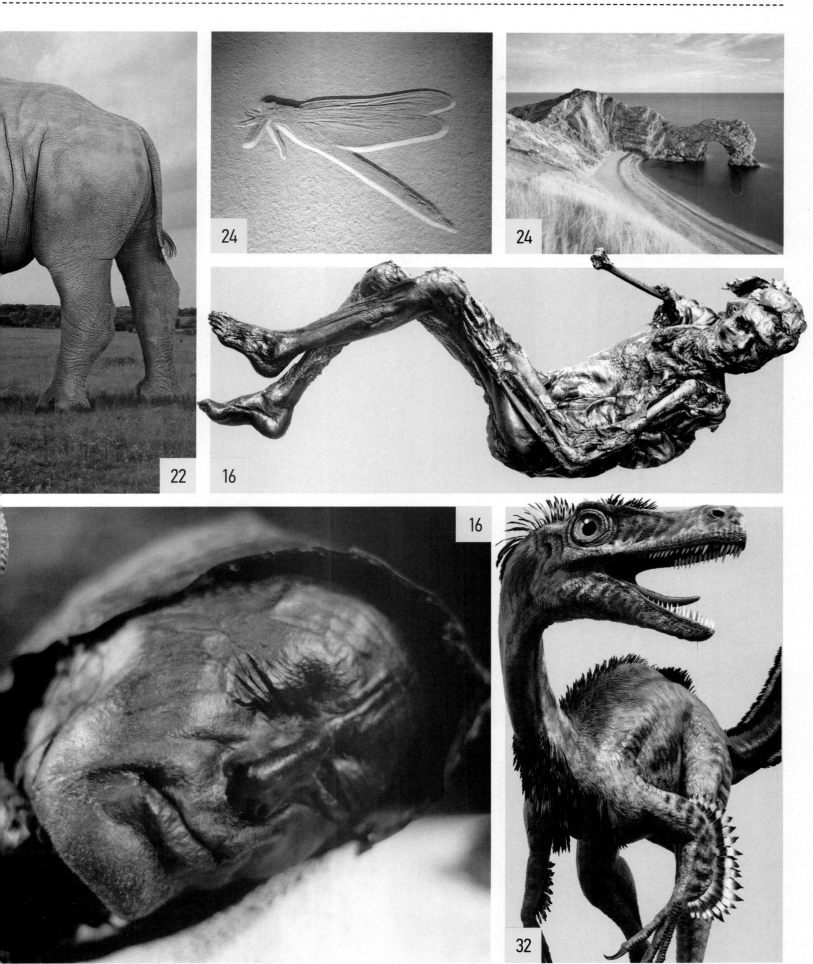

24

24

22

16

16

32

FROZ

IN TIME

THE INCREDIBLE WAYS NATURE HAS PRESERVED
PREHISTORIC HUMANS AND BEASTS FOR US TO FIND TODAY

Words by **Amy Grisdale**

EN

Image Source • Danish National Museum

BORREMOSE MAN
This body, dating from around 840 BCE, was found preserved in a peat bog in Denmark in 1946.

The Earth has experienced monumental changes since it was formed some 4.5 billion years ago. It has undergone alternating phases of cooling and warming, and this swinging between extremes of temperature dramatically changed the ecosystem. It brought about mass extinctions and the chance for new species to evolve in their place. The animals that ceased to exist left impressions, from partial footprints to intact fossilised skeletons. In some circumstances, however, animals of the past found their way into environments that preserved their entire bodies while the rest of the species rotted away.

One excellent method of animal preservation is freezing. Cold weather grinds the speed of organic decomposition to a halt by preventing the growth of bacteria that would otherwise feed on the decaying flesh. Temperatures were five to 22 degrees Celsius colder than today's climate in the most recent ice age. Animals were well-insulated with thick hair, such as the great woolly mammoth, or took shelter from the cold

Carcasses trapped in tar pits attracted carnivores, who also got stuck in the sticky substance

Image Source • Robert Bruce Horsfall

Tusk hunters are always on the trail of precious prehistoric ivory

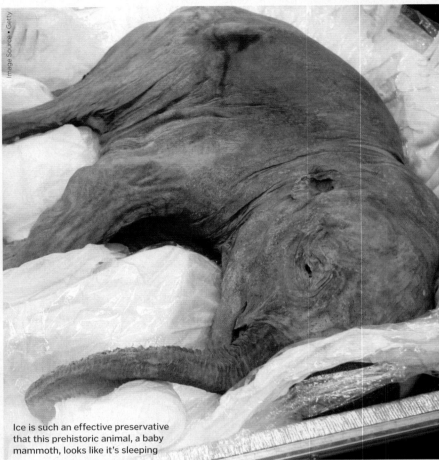

Ice is such an effective preservative that this prehistoric animal, a baby mammoth, looks like it's sleeping

like cave lions. Now most of the world has defrosted, but there are still areas that remain frozen, such as parts of Russia and Asia. Animals that lived and died in this bygone era have since been plucked from permafrost – a permanently frozen layer in the ground – with their bodies intact. A steppe bison that lived 36,000 years ago, for instance, was uncovered in pristine condition in 1979. Its rear end still bore the claw and tooth marks from the Ice Age lion that killed it.

Specimens that have survived thousands of years often became trapped somehow before a sudden plummet in temperature. The presence of food in the stomachs of Ice Age animals indicates that their bodies were frozen rapidly, preventing decay.

A large proportion of frozen remains are unearthed by miners on the hunt for precious metals. Scientists are invited to remove and study the remains, and they are able to draw conclusions about how the animal lived day to day and what may have led to its extinction. Scrutiny of a woolly rhino found by gold miners in northern Russia in 2007 convinced researchers that the species died out because its legs were too short to move efficiently through deep snow.

In the absence of ice, nature has other ways to preserve body tissue. An extremely important

> # "AN EXTREMELY IMPORTANT FACTOR IN PREVENTING DECOMPOSITION IS SEPARATION FROM OXYGEN"

factor in preventing decomposition is separation from oxygen. Europe's peat bogs have a magical combination of a lack of oxygen, low temperature and acidic water, which works to 'pickle' the remains of any animal that meets its end in the mud. Over time, layers of moss form on the bog's surface and release chemicals that halt bacterial growth.

Some of the most famous remnants of the past uncovered in these bogs are almost immaculately preserved human remains, along with a plethora of bizarre ancient artefacts that have been recovered in recent years. Huge hunks of an edible waxy substance are sometimes found with these 'peat-bog men' that are thought to be made of dairy or meat. This 'bog butter' may well have been a treasured food product to slather on Bronze Age bread. It's

TOLLUND MAN

A man was discovered in a bog near the Danish town of Tollund in such good condition that he was initially believed to be a recent murder victim. The body had been lying in rest for some 2,300 years, still dressed in primitive clothing. He appeared to indeed have been murdered, but the culprits themselves were long dead. Peat bogs may have been ancient grounds of burial or even ritual sacrifice. 'Tollund Man' was found with a braided leather cord wrapped tightly around his neck, and it's unclear whether he was hanged or strangled. The absence of trees across stretches of bog may have made people feel a connection to the heavens and therefore made it a place of religious significance.

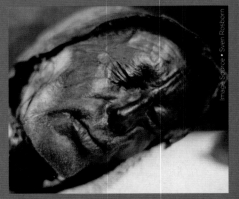

Tollund man is so well preserved, even his last facial expression is clear

BOG EMBALMING

CHEMICALS IN EUROPE'S BOG WATERS ARE A PERFECT MIX FOR PRESERVATION

RAISED BED
Elevated bogs contain the least oxygen but the most acid. These are the best at keeping a body fresh.

NO AIR
At depths of 30-50 centimetres (12-20 inches) there is no oxygen left in the acidic soil. Bacteria can't break the body down.

SPHAGNAN
Decaying moss releases a carbohydrate called sphagnan. This polymer extracts calcium from the bones, leaving the body soft and squishy.

UNDER PRESSURE
The weight of the water forces the peak soil to pack together tightly and nestle closely around the person.

Below: The Tollund Man was killed with this leather rope, and his hat is made of skin

Below: What was once sticky liquid tar now crumbles into easy-to-handle portions

TYPES OF FOSSILISATION

THERE ARE MANY WAYS ANIMALS AND PLANTS CAN BE PRESERVED OR ALTERED BY THE ENVIRONMENT

ASH
Clouds of volcanic ash bury remains of living beings without crushing or burning them, causing less damage. The remains of the city of Pompeii sat under a heap of ash for 1,669 years, and the people who had been buried by the ash were preserved with remarkably little alteration.

ICE
Ice is an amazing tool for preservation. No parts of the body are replaced when frozen. A normal human body can decompose in as little as eight years if it is buried in soil, whereas corpses are known to have lasted for 5,000 years or longer when they have been buried in ice.

ASPHALT
Crude oil seeps out of the ground, slowly forming pools on the surface. The oil becomes more viscous and sticky, trapping animals that come into contact with it. Bones that have soaked in tar are stained a tan colour, but otherwise are preserved without being affected by the environment.

CARBONISATION
The carbon in a soft-bodied animal creates an impression in sedimentary rock while the rest breaks down. A detailed carbon stamp remains on the surface, to be discovered later on. The majority of fossilised feathers are preserved as carbonised traces.

SEDIMENT
Mud sitting at the bottom of a lake or a river envelops carcasses of fish and invertebrates. It can accumulate and bury a dead animal very quickly, denying it oxygen and preserving the creature's flesh. Many millions of years can pass before it is once again exposed to the surface.

ASPHALT
Tree resin solidifies as amber, and animals can get stuck inside – just like the mosquitoes in *Jurassic Park*. Insect exoskeletons, made of the protein chitin, emerge almost unchanged. Unfortunately, however, the inner soft tissue is not preserved.

PEAT BOG
Around 100 bodies have been found preserved in peat bogs, a quarter of which are considered to be in exceptional condition. The remaining 75 that have been found are skeletons. They are from northern Europe, especially Ireland, the UK, Denmark, Germany and the Netherlands.

PETRIFICATION
This is the process through which organic material is slowly replaced by minerals. The remains are completely altered by this process, and the fossils that are produced are really stony replicas of the organic original.

possible that people of the past stored their butter in bogs to keep it cool and fresh, long before the days of refrigeration. It worked so well that this ancient spread is thought to still be edible – so long as the diner can ignore the smell.

Animals can get locked in a kind of time capsule by getting stuck in tar pits. In some parts of the world, springs of natural asphalt can seep up to the ground as thick crude oil. It accumulates and eventually forms a pool, the surface of which reacts with air to become thicker and stickier. We call these tar pits, and each one is a snapshot back in time. Prehistoric animals would get trapped and struggle to free

> ## "PREHISTORIC ANIMALS WOULD GET STUCK IN THE TAR AND STRUGGLE TO FREE THEMSELVES"

themselves. The resulting commotion would then attract predators, some of which would be lost in the tar themselves. Thousands of years later, the solidified tar began to be mined as asphalt, and the treasures within came to light.

La Brea is a world-renowned tar pit in Los Angeles, California. It trapped creatures for over 30,000 years, and new discoveries are still being made to this day. The site has been under excavation since 1913, and over 3.5 million specimens have been been found so far. More than 600 species of animals and plants have been identified from these remains, but most discoveries were bones of large animals. 90 per cent were carnivores like American lions and dire wolves – 4,000 of the latter have been retrieved from the tar, and some 400 of their skulls are on display at the George C Page Museum that stands on the excavation site.

Humans have learned so much from these pockets of prehistory. We have pieced together the events of evolution and have a detailed understanding of how we reached today. Chunks are missing, but areas that have preserved the past are helping us fill in the blanks.

The La Brea tar pit contains thousands of examples of preserved prehistoric creatures

Peat bogs, unremarkable at first glance, contain incredible pieces of history

HOW TAR PRESERVES PREHISTORIC ANIMALS

Low-grade crude oil seeps out of the ground, encountering air for the very first time. Contact with oxygen enables small and simple hydrocarbon chains to degrade or evaporate. As the lighter fractions of oil disappear, the remainder is purer and is less likely to escape. The tar begins to harden when it touches the cool air but remains viscous enough for a heavy animal to sink in.

Dust, leaves or even water can camouflage the tar's surface, making it easy for a wandering mastodon (a kind of prehistoric elephant) to stray into a natural vat of tar. It calls out to other members of its species for help, inadvertently alerting wolves and big cats to its plight. Even if it dies of starvation or dehydration, it takes up to 20 weeks to sink. During this time, it is visited by hungry predators that are then at risk of getting stuck themselves.

The George C Page Museum opened in 1977, and an excavation is underway that has the potential to double its collection

FIVE INCREDIBLE ICE MUMMIES

These frozen prehistoric animals are superbly well-preserved and they are now famous around the world

Sasha
This woolly rhino baby was the first young member of its species ever found. It's unclear if it is male or female, but the horn size suggests it had been weaned by the time it died. It roamed the mammoth steppe, a dry, cold region from Spain to Siberia.

Image Source • Getty

Lion or lynx
A squashed, mummified cat was unearthed in eastern Siberia in 2017. It could either be a lynx kitten or a cave lion cub. Its coat is in beautiful condition, but we aren't sure of the species as we simply don't know what a cave lion truly looked like.

Image Source • Mauricio Antón

Death by drowning
Mammoths from 40,000 years ago have been studied via CT scans. The results showed that two calves, recovered from different regions of Siberia, had both choked on mud. They otherwise appeared plump and healthy.

Image Source • Vasyatkal

Old but good
The most complete steppe bison specimen ever found is 9,000 years old. It has a complete heart, brain and digestive system, along with near-perfect blood vessels. Some organs have shrunk over time but are remarkable nonetheless.

Image Source • Bernt Rostad

Frozen foal
A two-month-old horse was found buried approximately 100 metres (328 feet) deep in a Siberian crater. In life it stood almost one metre (three feet) tall, and its hooves are still intact, along with tiny hairs that are still visible inside the foal's nostrils.

Image Source • James St. John

TITANIC RHINO ANCESTORS

WHAT IT LACKED IN WEAPONRY, THE PARACERATHERIUM MADE UP FOR IN SHEER SIZE

A ppearing over the horizon or emerging from a patch of trees, Paraceratherium would be an intimidating and somewhat confusing sight to a modern observer: with the height of a dinosaur and the leathery skin of an elephant, it wouldn't be immediately apparent what these creatures were.

Paraceratherium, scientists now know, was a genus of giant rhino. The group contained towering beasts standing almost five metres (16 feet) tall at the shoulder and potentially weighing 20,000 kilograms (22 tons). Its members lived across Eurasia during the Oligocene epoch, between 34 and 23 million years ago, and were so far back in the branches of the rhino family tree that they predate the evolution of the facial horn.

Paraceratherium's exact height isn't agreed on because the fossils that form our knowledge of the genus are incomplete, but with its estimated size it's a strong contender for the title of largest land mammal ever. While rhinos today are more compact, Paraceratherium's legs and neck were relatively long. This impressive body allowed the rhinos to browse tall trees and navigate huge ranges in search of food and mates. To grab hold of foliage, it had a muscular top lip or perhaps even a proboscis like a tapir. Unlike their solitary modern relatives, it's thought that females and their calves travelled and lived together in small herds.

Despite its size, Paraceratherium was not invincible. Bite marks on fossils suggest that some young and ill animals fell victim to enormous crocodiles, and the entire genus went extinct after about 11 million years on Earth. Elephant-like animals emerging on Eurasia could have reduced the food available to the rhinos by destroying areas of forest, and large predators moving north from Africa may have been able to prey on Paraceratherium calves. The cause of their extinction is unknown, but it's likely that several factors contributed to the downfall of this graceful giant.

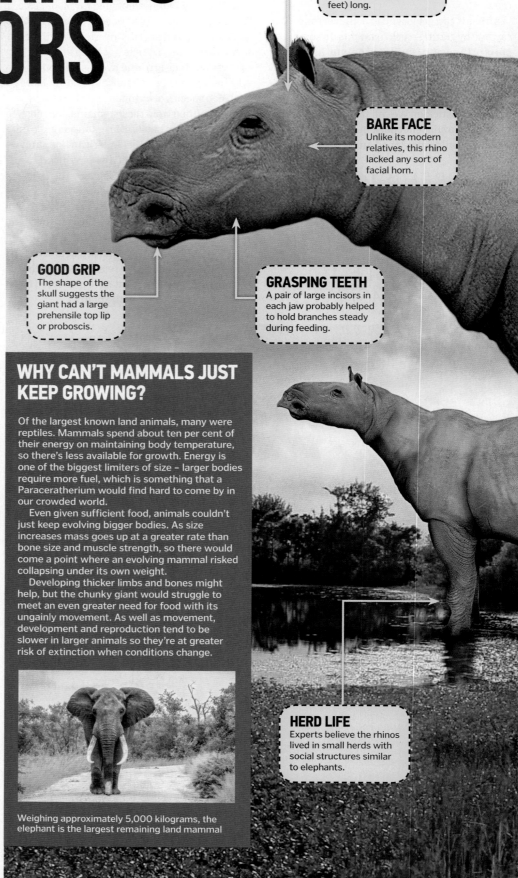

HEFTY HEAD
Supported by a long neck, Paraceratherium's skull was about 1.3 metres (4.3 feet) long.

BARE FACE
Unlike its modern relatives, this rhino lacked any sort of facial horn.

GOOD GRIP
The shape of the skull suggests the giant had a large prehensile top lip or proboscis.

GRASPING TEETH
A pair of large incisors in each jaw probably helped to hold branches steady during feeding.

HERD LIFE
Experts believe the rhinos lived in small herds with social structures similar to elephants.

WHY CAN'T MAMMALS JUST KEEP GROWING?

Of the largest known land animals, many were reptiles. Mammals spend about ten per cent of their energy on maintaining body temperature, so there's less available for growth. Energy is one of the biggest limiters of size – larger bodies require more fuel, which is something that a Paraceratherium would find hard to come by in our crowded world.

Even given sufficient food, animals couldn't just keep evolving bigger bodies. As size increases mass goes up at a greater rate than bone size and muscle strength, so there would come a point where an evolving mammal risked collapsing under its own weight.

Developing thicker limbs and bones might help, but the chunky giant would struggle to meet an even greater need for food with its ungainly movement. As well as movement, development and reproduction tend to be slower in larger animals so they're at greater risk of extinction when conditions change.

Weighing approximately 5,000 kilograms, the elephant is the largest remaining land mammal

"DESPITE ITS SIZE, PARACERATHERIUM WAS NOT INVINCIBLE"

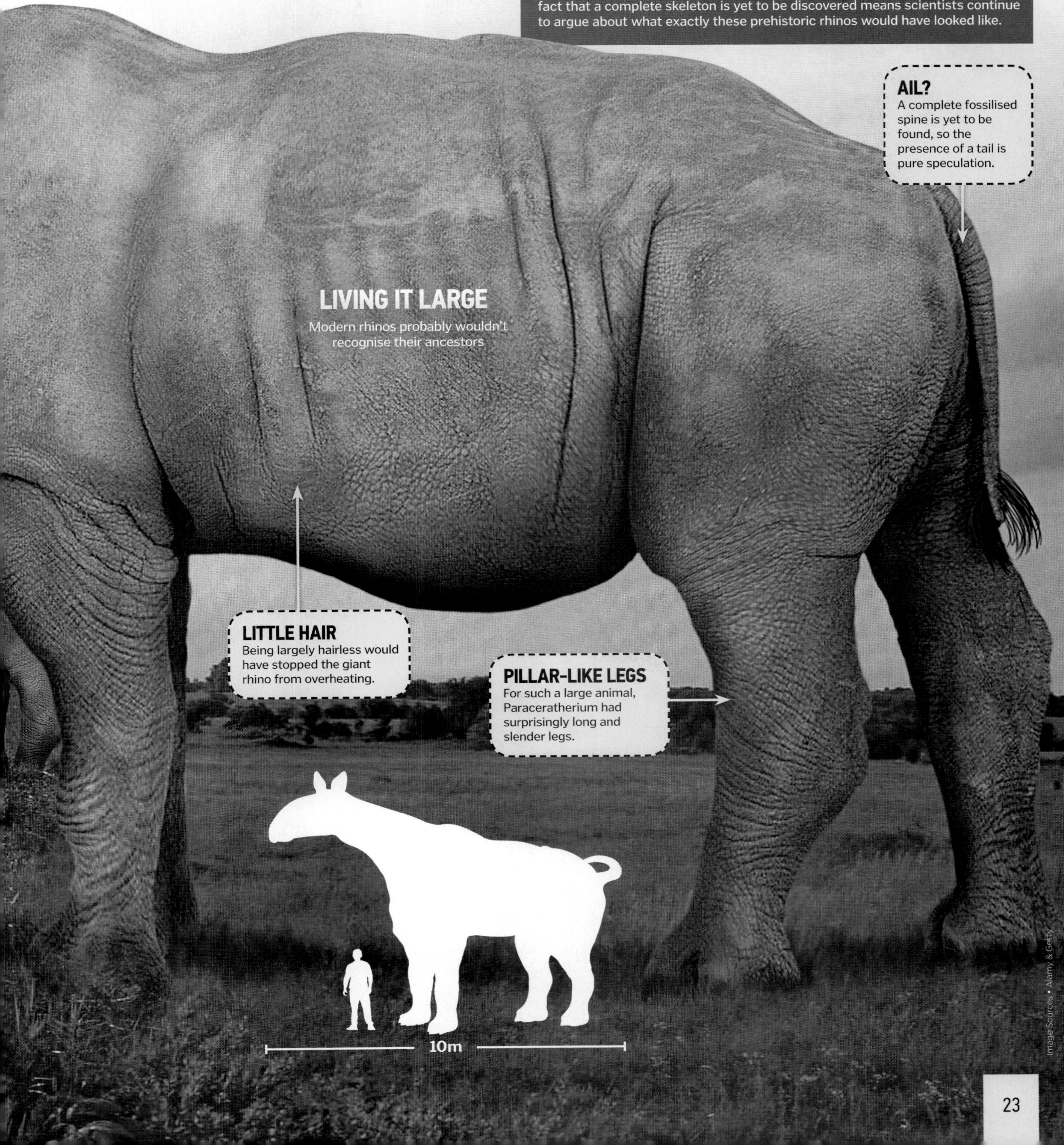

LARGE BUT LITTLE-KNOWN

Relatively little is known about Paraceratherium. The first fossils now recognised as belonging to the genus were collected in Balochistan (modern-day Pakistan) in 1907–08 by a British geologist. Other fossils began to turn up across Asia but political unrest and global conflict meant that collaboration on research into an extinct rhino genus wasn't exactly a priority, so discoveries were published in local languages and not shared. The correct taxonomy of members of Paraceratherium and their close relatives is still debated, and the fact that a complete skeleton is yet to be discovered means scientists continue to argue about what exactly these prehistoric rhinos would have looked like.

AIL?
A complete fossilised spine is yet to be found, so the presence of a tail is pure speculation.

LIVING IT LARGE
Modern rhinos probably wouldn't recognise their ancestors

LITTLE HAIR
Being largely hairless would have stopped the giant rhino from overheating.

PILLAR-LIKE LEGS
For such a large animal, Paraceratherium had surprisingly long and slender legs.

10m

Image Sources • Alamy & Getty

23

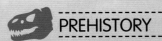
THE JURA

The power of the ocean created Lulworth Cove around 10,000 years ago

Image Source • Pixabay

"ANIMALS AND PLANTS HAVE BEEN IMMORTALISED IN THE ROCK AS FOSSILS, CREATING A UNIQUE RECORD OF PREHISTORIC LIFE"

SSIC COAST

THE LAYERS OF ROCK HOLDING THE SECRETS TO 185 MILLION YEARS OF NATURAL HISTORY

The Jurassic Coast is the only place on the planet where 185 million years of the Earth's history is preserved and exposed in layers of rock. Stretching 154 kilometres across the south coast of England, it is home to spectacular geographic formations and wildlife, and it has been the location of many of the most important fossil finds in scientific history. Between the dramatic cliffs, secluded coves and magnificent coastal stacks, an immeasurable number of animals and plants have been immortalised in the rock as fossils, creating a unique record of prehistoric life.

Throughout its history, the Jurassic Coast has been a desert, a shallow tropical sea and a marshland. Debris from each of these environments has turned into layers of rock, with the oldest at the bottom and the youngest on the surface. Over millions of years, animals and plants have died here, becoming buried and trapped within the rock layers, which now provide us with a record of life from the Triassic, Jurassic and Cretaceous periods.

As the cliffs have been eroded by the tides over the years, a cross-section of the rock strata has been appeared, allowing us to see the banding of rock from different times. Originally stacked horizontally, tectonic movements have caused the strata to become tilted, which has created a unique 'walk through time' going from west to east.

The coast starts with the 250-million-year-old dusty red rocks and ends with 65-million-year-old white chalk cliffs, with fossil-rich Jurassic grey clay and pastel limestone situated in the middle of the coastline. Each part of the coast now serves as a rare snapshot in time, telling pieces of a story through its rock formations and the fossilised remains of the plants and animals that thrived during that period.

A WALK THROUGH TIME

The story starts at the far western tip of Orcombe Point. Made of layers of red mudstone and sandstone first laid down when the coast was a desert at the start of the Triassic period, this desert era was almost completely devoid of life

Image Source • Getty

25

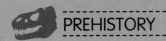

JURASSIC COAST ON THE MAP

HUNTING FOR HISTORY ALONG ENGLAND'S SOUTH COAST

WEST DORSET

LYME REGIS
Coastal erosion regularly exposes new fossils in this region, particularly from the Jurassic period.

ORCOMBE POINT
The red mudstone and sandstone of the cliffs here were laid down in the Triassic period when the region was a desert.

WEST BAY

SEATOWN
The cliffs here date back to the early Jurassic period, when most of Europe was covered by a shallow sea.

EXMOUTH

as it followed the largest known mass extinction event, which led to 75 per cent of species on Earth dying out. The catastrophic impact means this area doesn't contain fossils. The Jurassic Coast then turns to the beautiful banded grey Blue Lias rocks, that are scattered with limestone ledges and green ammonite mudstone. It is in this middle section of the Jurassic Coast that you can find beaches abundant in fossils, with different locations hosting different specimens, including dragonflies, shrimps and sharks.

The famous Lyme Regis beach can be found here, with 71 different rock strata identified, each with its own species of ammonite. Other beaches include Seatown, which is bountiful in the fine-grained sandstone known as the Eype Starfish Bed, home to a sea of perfectly preserved brittle stars. Then there's Burton Bradstock, where shark fins, echinoids and brachiopods are all waiting to be discovered.

Finally, there are the youngest rocks on the Jurassic Coast, which are situated at the furthest eastern point. This soft, white, crumbly rock is the crushed remains of the skeletons of tiny marine animals from approximately 100 million years ago. In the Cretaceous period the coast was submerged in a warm tropical sea, where an immeasurable number of microscopic plankton swarmed. As these creatures died, their skeletons, made from calcium carbonate, gradually accumulated on the seafloor, creating a thick blanket of chalk.

After this time, the Mesozoic era came to a dramatic end when a ten-kilometre- (6.2-mile-) wide asteroid plummeted into the Gulf of Mexico, causing cataclysmic devastation that wiped out 75 per cent of all life on Earth. This was the end of the dinosaurs, but it wasn't all doom and gloom. The extinction of the dinosaurs paved the way for new species to evolve, including us.

FINDING YOUR OWN FANTASTIC FOSSILS

FIND THE RIGHT ROCKS
Fossils can only be found in certain rocks, known as sedimentary rocks, because they indicate favourable conditions for fossil forming. These rocks are made from a combination of sand, silt and the skeletal remains of dead animals, and they tend to have formed as a result of rivers, lakes or resting on the seafloor. The good news is the Jurassic Coast contains lots of sedimentary rock, which means lots of fossils.

The types of sedimentary rock you will find on the Jurassic Coast include shale, made from hardened mud, and limestone, which is mostly made from microscopic marine skeletons. When you are looking for your own fossils, make sure that you know there is sedimentary rock in your fossil-hunting location.

CHECK THE LAW
In general, if the fossil is still within its original position (either within the cliff or bedrock) then it should not be collected as it could potentially cause damage to the area. Otherwise, in most places you are free to go and hunt for fossils. Make sure that you research the specific area you will be visiting to ensure you are not breaking the law.

STAY SAFE
Always go fossil hunting as the tide is going out, and be careful not to get too close to crumbling cliffs. Sedimentary rock can collapse quite easily, causing landslides or rocks to fall from the side of the cliff. Remember to tell someone where you are going and take a friend or parent with you, and don't rely on your mobile phone because you might not have any signal.

GEOLOGICAL FORMATIONS
How the forces of nature carved these rocky landmarks

Old Harry's Rock
Old Harry's Rock was once part of a stretch of chalk between Purbeck and the Isle of Wight. The other parts of the stretch have been eroded by the ocean, causing caves and arches to form. Heavy rain and wind caused the collapse of the top of the arches, leaving disconnected stacks of the white rock.

Chesil Bank
This spectacular natural phenomena is a barrier beach – a narrow section of sand that is separated from the mainland by a body of water. Chesil Bank has been rolled by the sea towards the land to join the mainland with the Isle of Portland.

Lulworth Crumple
The concordant and discordant coastline has created movement that is evident in the rocks. The continents crashed together millions of years ago, causing layers of rock to become folded and twisted, eventually buckling under the pressure.

EAST DORSET

BURTON BRADSTOCK
Ammonite fossils are a common find in this area, mostly dating back to the mid-Jurassic.

OLD HARRY ROCKS
Skeletons of plankton that died during the Cretaceous formed the chalk found here over millions of years.

URDLE DOOR
This natural arch was formed around 25 million years ago when the African and European tectonic plates collided.

PURBECK

WAREHAM

WEYMOUTH

WEST LULWORTH

SWANAGE

Seatown is a quiet fossil-hunting beach on the Jurassic Coast

"SHARK FINS, ECHINOIDS AND BRACHIOPODS ARE ALL WAITING TO BE DISCOVERED"

Image Source • Alamy

HOW DOES A FOSSIL FORM?

Fossilisation can usually only occur under very specific conditions, somewhere the organism won't get eaten by scavengers. This is more likely to happen when an animal or plant dies in a watery environment like an ocean or a lake. Mud and silt cover the dead organism and over time the soft parts (such as the internal organs, muscle and skin) decay and rot away. The bones and shells are left behind in the mud. Eventually, the mud is covered with sediment, which hardens into rock. As the trapped bones then start to decay, minerals seep into the space they have left behind cell by cell. This is called petrification. If the bones completely decay, the cavity in the rock left behind can be completely filled with minerals to create a stone replica.

Other fossils can be formed when insects become trapped in tree sap, which hardens and forms amber. Animals can also get trapped in the mix of hot gas and ash that results from a volcanic eruption.

FINDING OUT ALL ABOUT FOSSILS

From flies to fish, discover how to identify your prehistoric finds

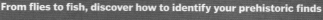

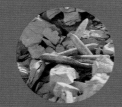

Ammonites
Ammonites are the most common fossils on the Jurassic Coast. They were squid-like animals and their fossils are usually a ribbed spiral shape.

Belemnites
Belemnites were closely related to ammonites. They had large eyes and an ink sac, with hard beaks and tail fins, plus ten arms with hooks to grab prey.

Echinoids
Echinoids have been around for about 530 million years. Many had a hard shell with spines and a beak of five teeth. They can still be found with spines intact.

Fish
Lots of fish can be found on the Jurassic Coast, but they don't resemble those we recognise today because they were covered in a hard enamel shell.

Insects
Around since before the dinosaurs, insects have an external skeleton (exoskeleton), and this is usually the part that is fossilised.

Image Source • Pixabay

Ammonites are a relatively common find along the Jurassic Coast

The best finds come when you start splitting rocks open, like this huge septarian nodule

TAKE EQUIPMENT

If you can get one, use a high-quality splitting tool to crack open rocks. A hammer and cold steel chisel combination is ideal, preferably a large chisel for completing the bulk of the work then a smaller chisel for the finer work and removing the fossil from the rock. If it is not possible to get your hands on this equipment, you can just use a hammer. Either way, remember to take goggles to protect your eyes from rock splinters. Other equipment that might be helpful are a pen and paper for labelling your rocks, and some plastic bags to store them in. It's also a good idea to record the date and location you found your fossil.

FIND A NODULE

Start looking through the rocks and pebbles beneath the cliff and further towards the ocean. Keep your eyes peeled for regular, round-shaped rocks called nodules. Often you will see nodules with regular lines and patterns on the surface of the pebble that sometimes look like stripes. These will mostly be around the middle.

No two nodules are exactly the same, though, so sometimes you might see an ammonite already poking out of the stone, or you might catch a glimpse of the white zigzags as an edge of a shell starts to show.

Place the nodule somewhere where it can't move and then hit it smoothly and confidently in the middle. It should split open, and with some practice you will be able to learn how to do this in a way that opens the nodule symmetrically and keeps the fossil intact.

AFTER YOU FIND YOUR FOSSIL

So, you've made a great fossil find. Now what? It's important to research to see if your fossil is scientifically important. There are lots of

A FOSSIL-HUNTING PIONEER

MARY ANNING
21 MAY 1799 – 9 MARCH 1847

Mary Anning was an English amateur palaeontologist. She taught herself how to find fossils and became an expert at removing them from the rock without causing damage, becoming world-famous for her discoveries of Jurassic marine fossils at Lyme Regis. Her work was so significant that it changed the way we understand prehistoric life and the history of our planet.

She would head out in dangerous conditions in the winter looking for fossils after parts of the cliff had fallen away. In 1812, Anning found her most important discovery – an almost complete Ichthyosaurus. She followed this up in 1823 with the discovery of a complete Plesiosaurus. Her work can still be found in museums around the world, including the Natural History Museum in London.

Mary Anning's finds changed our understanding of prehistoric life

Some top tips from junior fossil hunters Ella and Olivia

"If you have a small, dark grey rock with white lines around it then probably you might find an ammonite in it or an amber stone"
Ella

"Find one like this – it's called a beer. You have to find one with white lines around it and it should be sort of flat and round"
Olivia

Q&A WITH AN AMATEUR FOSSIL HUNTER

ANTHONY STONESTREET IS A HUMANITIES STUDENT AT CARDIFF UNIVERSITY WHO HAS BEEN FOSSIL HUNTING IN THE UK SINCE HE WAS SEVEN

When was the first time you went fossil hunting?
It would have been in the summer of 2006 at Lyme Regis in Dorset. I remember finding a few pieces, they were mainly fragments that I found lying on the beach. We were only passing through and I happened to notice the town's Welcome sign, which has a huge ammonite plastered on it. So we stopped and headed down to the beach.

How often have you returned to Lyme Regis?
Plenty of times! My most recent visit was in March. Not all excursions are successful, though.

Have you had any success on the other beaches on the Jurassic Coast?
I've been to Charmouth – the people in the Heritage Centre are great if you need anything identified. My favourite location on the Dorset coast has to be Seatown, the next hamlet along. It's a mixed bag when it comes to what you might find, but it can yield some really nice fossils.

What have you found in Seatown?
I once found a relatively large ammonite there. Someone had already had a go at it before me, and I just found it as it was on a boulder. I'd say it was about six centimetres (2.4 inches) in diameter.

What's your best find in the Jurassic Coast?
Probably a pyrite ammonite I found at Charmouth. It was a decent size and so far it hasn't disintegrated – plus it stands out from the rest. I did once find a coral segment at Lulworth Cove; it wasn't that big, but it did have an interesting pattern on it. I've found some pretty large belemnite segments and a few whole ones.

How does the Jurassic Coast compare to other sites in the UK?
The Lyme Regis area is one of the most accessible coastal locations in the country, but due to sheer popularity the best finds are gone quite quickly. In comparison, the Yorkshire coast is less well known for its fossils, but compared to Dorset, the locations are harder to access.

Do you have any tips?
For me, finding the best fossil involves going where other people are less likely to have gone before, all the while making sure the area is safe.

When you get to the site, what do you do?
No matter where you happen to go, I think it's best to go when new material is made available. Go on a receding tide and when the cliff is crumbling on a regular basis, not when it's about to collapse in one huge chunk. In either situation, remember to keep a safe distance from the cliff.

First of all, I try figuring out where the rubble is or where the scree slopes are. Once I get there, I try to see if I can find any loose bits of material lying on the surface or in large boulders. From there, I try to find a smaller piece I can break apart and then see what I can find.

Are there any clues to what pieces might contain a fossil? Like a certain shape?
On the Yorkshire coast it'll be round, dark brown or black nodules, which can contain some great ammonites. On the Jurassic Coast it'll be banded pieces of light-grey sediment.

What's your favourite find ever?
That has to be a really large ammonite I found on the Yorkshire coast some years ago. It was about ten centimetres (four inches) in diameter.

What do you like about fossil hunting?
It's calm; you're often alone on the beach. And you don't know what you're going to find, if anything. There's an element of chance to it.

Do you have any final words of advice for our readers who might want to get started in fossil hunting themselves?
You're more likely to make a good find in winter or after a storm. If you stick to all the safety rules, there's no reason you won't find something.

With some practice, it is possible to crack open rocks perfectly to reveal fossils

Some of Anthony's best finds over the last ten years

Image Source • Theodore Gray (Nautiloid.net)

The famous chalk sea stacks of Old Harry's Rock

databases to do this online. You should also consider if you need to soak your fossil in water to protect it from salt damage. Once you have done this you can start using smaller tools to remove the last bits of rock. You could even get a magnifying glass to help do this bit.

"THROUGHOUT ITS HISTORY THE JURASSIC COAST HAS BEEN A DESERT, A SHALLOW TROPICAL SEA AND A MARSHLAND"

Far right
Exposed rock strata along the Jurassic Coast reveal millions of years of geological history

THE HISTORIC BEACHES OF THE JURASSIC COAST

Our team took a day out of the office to visit some of the beaches on the Jurassic Coast. Our first stop was Lyme Regis, which we absolutely loved for fossil hunting. We walked across the beach until we found lots of other people who were looking for fossils. Some were real experts, while others were just trying fossil collecting for the first time, but everyone was working together and comparing their finds with one another.

It didn't take very long before we found some ammonite fossils ourselves. It is a huge beach with beautiful cliffs, and when the tide is out there are plenty of places to look. We didn't crack open any rocks (someone forgot to bring the hammer with them), but we did find huge ammonites just imprinted into the rocks along the shoreline.

If you want somewhere a bit quieter, our favourite beach was Burton Bradstock, which was a much more relaxing environment. It also had a truly stunning display of colourful yellow rock strata. But this beach rewards the patient. We didn't have any luck finding any fossils, but we did notice lots ammonite nodules in the cliff, so there must be a treasure trove buried underneath waiting to be found.

Lyme Regis is a prime fossil-hunting spot along the coast and was once home to famous palaeontologist Mary Anning

CONSERVING THE COAST

The Jurassic Coast has survived a lot through its history, but now its future depends on us. The biggest threat to its geography and fossils is the ocean and how we choose to manage its effect on the cliffs. Conservation of the site relies on allowing the ocean to continue the natural process of erosion and deposition, as this is what has created the beautiful coastline. However, this same coastline is at risk due to human activity.

If coastal defences such as seawalls are constructed to prevent erosion, they will start to interfere with nature, and in an attempt to stabilise the cliffs, promote the growth of vegetation, which would obscure toe fossils and rock strata. The conservation of the Jurassic Coast will always rely on a balancing act between the ocean and the cliffs, as well as the management of beach litter and shipping traffic.

The sea has shaped the Jurassic Coast as we know it today

HOW DO WE KNOW DINOSAURS HAD FEATHERS?

IT TURNS OUT THAT FOSSILS HAVE PRESERVED MUCH MORE THAN JUST BONE STRUCTURE

Most of us have been captivated by the idea of dinosaurs since childhood. Among their numbers stood veracious hunters, towering leaf-eaters, armoured warriors and soaring giants. Add to that the wonder that we all felt when we learned that our planet used to belong to them, that before we inherited the (self-awarded) title of Earth's apex animal, it was the reptilian dinosaurs that ruled supreme.

In films, books and other illustrations, we long envisaged dinosaurs to be clad in scales and thick skin, much like the reptiles of today – such as the terrifying yet magnificent Komodo dragon. A fearsome appearance such as this, after all, is only fitting for a world-conquering

group. But would our perception of dinosaurs be altered if we were to learn that some were feathered and some were even fluffy?

Scientists found the first evidence of feathered dinosaurs over 150 years ago with the discovery of the Archaeopteryx. After the animal died, it left behind an immensely well-preserved fossil, and tucked beneath its long arms were the impressions of many familiar curved shapes. The evidence was clear for all to see – the Archaeopteryx had feathers.

It wasn't until the 1990s, however, that scientists would uncover much more evidence that showed that Archaeopteryx wasn't alone in its feathery ways. Archaeologists in China unearthed a collection of complete fossils that

had a clear halo of 'dino fuzz' surrounding the skeletal impressions, which they determined must had been a form of primitive feathers, or perhaps fur.

The modern expert opinion holds that an entire group of dinosaurs, known as the Theropods, likely bore feathers in some capacity. These would have started as fluffy, primitive barbs, but in some species would have evolved into fully established feathered wings that were sometimes even used for flying. Perhaps most intriguingly, the beloved velociraptor and the Tyrannosaurus rex belonged to this group, so these terrifying creatures may have actually looked much more 'cuddly' than was previously believed.

THE COLOUR MYSTERY SOLVED

We may now know that many dinosaurs were adorned with some sort of feathered coat, but what colours were they? If we look to today's avian descendants of the dinosaurs, birds, we see a spectrum of coloured plumage used to perform a bunch of different functions, such as camouflage and attracting a mate. But with limited insight into the behaviour of different dinosaur species, we can only make educated guesses as to how these factors could have contributed to the colour of their feathers.

Fortunately, precious fossil evidence lends us concrete proof of the colours worn by dinosaurs – for some colours, at least. Using sophisticated microscopes, in well-preserved fossils we can identify impressions of pigment molecules that have been preserved for tens of millions of years.

These pigments have well-defined shapes that are responsible for particular colours, which enable scientists to determine if a dinosaur's feathers bore this hue. We can also compare the structures of these ancient pigments against modern-day birds, allowing us to unlock the secrets of the past by using the present.

FEATHERED FAMILY TREE

Theropod feathers evolved to help dinosaurs in a variety of ways, from disguise to flight. So who was in the family?

Filament
Protofeathers were composed of single hollow filaments. These would then later evolve into established feathers in many species.

Tuft
Protofeathers evolved into tufts of several filaments, giving dinosaurs a halo of fluff either in patches or a full coat.

Barbs
Over many generations, tufts would have transformed into more rigid and organised structures of barbs connected to a central shaft.

Feather
Eventually, barbs would have been crosslinked by structures known as barbules, producing advanced feathers capable of supporting full flight.

Right This is one idea of what a Deinonychus may have looked like, complete with feathers

DINOSAURS

BASAL ARCHOSAURS

CROCS   PTEROSAURS

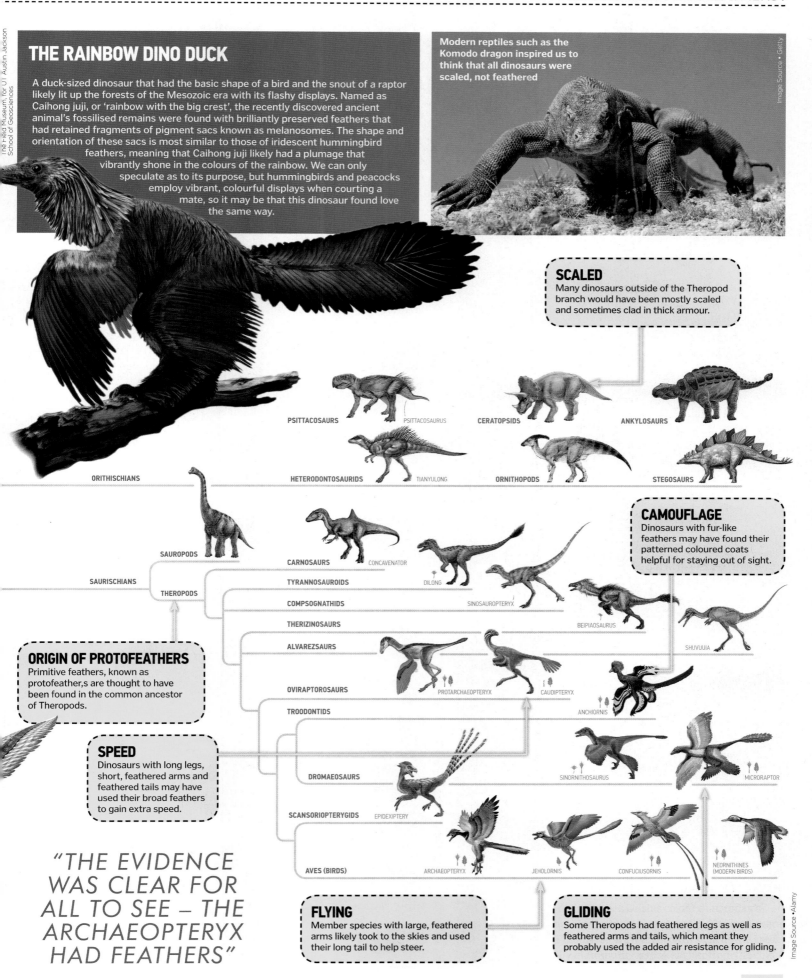

THE RAINBOW DINO DUCK

A duck-sized dinosaur that had the basic shape of a bird and the snout of a raptor likely lit up the forests of the Mesozoic era with its flashy displays. Named as Caihong juji, or 'rainbow with the big crest', the recently discovered ancient animal's fossilised remains were found with brilliantly preserved feathers that had retained fragments of pigment sacs known as melanosomes. The shape and orientation of these sacs is most similar to those of iridescent hummingbird feathers, meaning that Caihong juji likely had a plumage that vibrantly shone in the colours of the rainbow. We can only speculate as to its purpose, but hummingbirds and peacocks employ vibrant, colourful displays when courting a mate, so it may be that this dinosaur found love the same way.

Modern reptiles such as the Komodo dragon inspired us to think that all dinosaurs were scaled, not feathered

Image Source • Getty

The Field Museum, for UI / Austin Jackson School of Geosciences

SCALED
Many dinosaurs outside of the Theropod branch would have been mostly scaled and sometimes clad in thick armour.

PSITTACOSAURS — PSITTACOSAURUS

CERATOPSIDS

ANKYLOSAURS

ORITHISCHIANS

HETERODONTOSAURIDS — TIANYULONG

ORNITHOPODS

STEGOSAURS

CAMOUFLAGE
Dinosaurs with fur-like feathers may have found their patterned coloured coats helpful for staying out of sight.

SAUROPODS

SAURISCHIANS

THEROPODS

CARNOSAURS — CONCAVENATOR

TYRANNOSAUROIDS — DILONG

COMPSOGNATHIDS — SINOSAUROPTERYX

THERIZINOSAURS — BEIPIAOSAURUS

ALVAREZSAURS — SHUVUUIA

ORIGIN OF PROTOFEATHERS
Primitive feathers, known as protofeather,s are thought to have been found in the common ancestor of Theropods.

OVIRAPTOROSAURS — PROTARCHAEOPTERYX — CAUDIPTERYX

ANCHIORNIS

TROODONTIDS

SPEED
Dinosaurs with long legs, short, feathered arms and feathered tails may have used their broad feathers to gain extra speed.

DROMAEOSAURS — SINORNITHOSAURUS — MICRORAPTOR

SCANSORIOPTERYGIDS — EPIDEXIPTERY

"THE EVIDENCE WAS CLEAR FOR ALL TO SEE – THE ARCHAEOPTERYX HAD FEATHERS"

AVES (BIRDS) — ARCHAEOPTERYX — JEHOLORNIS — CONFUCIUSORNIS — NEORNITHINES (MODERN BIRDS)

FLYING
Member species with large, feathered arms likely took to the skies and used their long tail to help steer.

GLIDING
Some Theropods had feathered legs as well as feathered arms and tails, which meant they probably used the added air resistance for gliding.

Image Source •Alamy

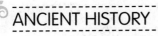

ANCIENT HISTORY

36

50

42

44

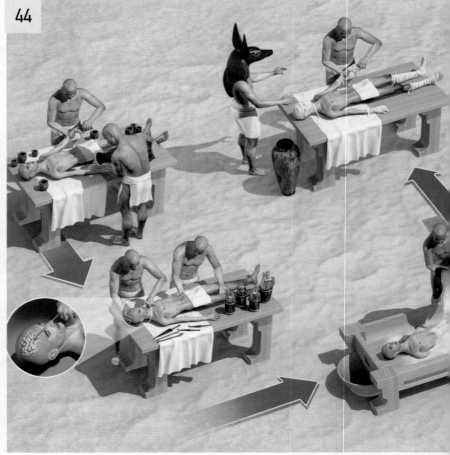

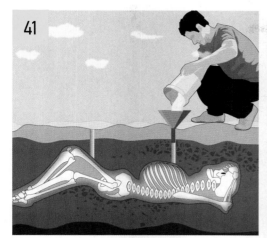

41

40

36

40

41

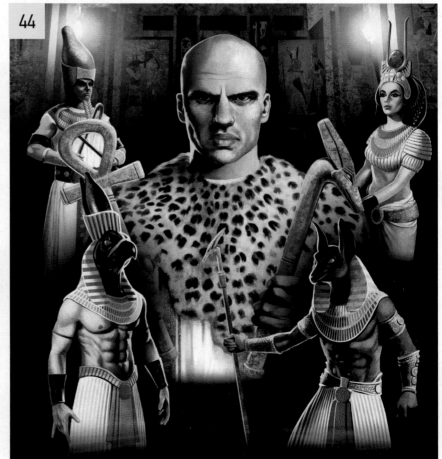

44

Image Source • Joe Cummings

LIFE IN THE LEGION

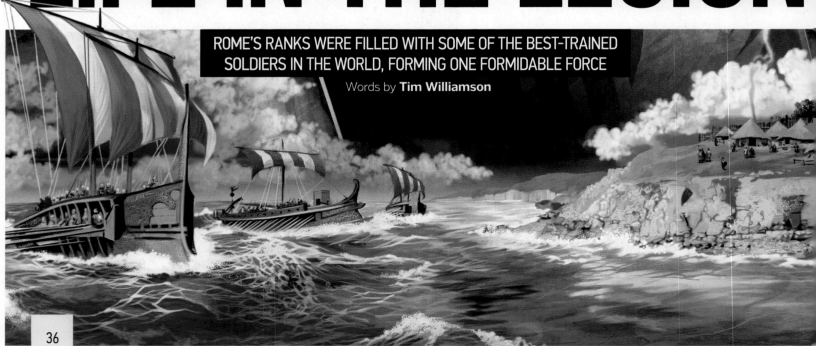

ROME'S RANKS WERE FILLED WITH SOME OF THE BEST-TRAINED
SOLDIERS IN THE WORLD, FORMING ONE FORMIDABLE FORCE

Words by **Tim Williamson**

Roman armies were highly organised and supremely disciplined entities of war. Each legion numbered around 5,000 men, all trained and armed to defeat enemies from all across the vast Roman territories. The backbone of a legion was its legionaries, heavy infantry with sworn allegiance to the Senate and the people of Rome, and later to the emperor. However, the daily lives of these men weren't filled with glorious adventures fighting Rome's enemies but were instead governed by strict routine, endless hours of marching and yet more hours spent training.

As a legionary, you would march, work, eat, fight and rest alongside the men of your contubernium, or squad. Each contubernium contained eight soldiers, with ten contubernia making up one centuria. At the end of each day's march, after constructing the legion's fortifications for the night, each squad would set up its own tent, then enjoy some precious down time. One servant was assigned to each squad, who would repair kit, cook, clean and carry out any general chores for the soldiers. At least one member of each squad would be assigned to guard duty throughout the night, before the camp rose at the crack of dawn and prepared to march once more.

TRAINING AND DRILLS

Officers trained their men mercilessly, using techniques and combat styles developed by gladiators. Experience of the competitive and bloody contests in the arenas had made gladiator trainers experts in teaching fighters how to best their opponents. New recruits practised with wooden swords and shields, which were heavier than the equipment they would be armed with in a battle. This was intended to build up strength and stamina for

These reenactors are playing the role of auxiliary cavalry, armed with spears and longer swords for cutting down the enemy

the real fight. Practising on wooden stakes, recruits repeated drills to strike at the head, legs and torso areas, all while dodging and blocking as if their lives depended on it.

The next stage of training was the armatura, a sparring exercise that pitched two soldiers head-to-head. Wielding blunted or covered blades to avoid injury, they attacked and parried one another using the same techniques learned fighting the wooden stakes. Legionaries trained in this way throughout their careers so as to maintain their skills. In fact, it was so important that buildings were constructed especially for this purpose, so practice could continue regardless of the weather. Those who underperformed during training were punished with reduced rations, heavy fines or even a rough beating from an officer.

Weakness or dissent in the ranks could mean the difference between victory and defeat on the battlefield, so strict discipline was often enforced through harsh punishments. Depending on the circumstances, crimes such as theft, desertion or even falling asleep on duty could be met with a whipping, demotion or even public execution – usually by being clubbed to death. In very rare circumstances where entire units ran away in the face of the enemy, the sentence of decimation was carried out – one in every ten of the accused would be executed. The fear of such a fate was usually enough to bolster the courage of any wavering squad or centuria

BLOOD AND COIN

A regular wage was one of the key attractions for recruits, and legionaries were the highest-paid units in the army. Through promotion and time served, soldiers could hope to receive pay-and-a-half (sesquiplicarius), and veteran troops eventually could get double pay (duplicarius).

> "OFFICERS TRAINED THEIR MEN USING GLADIATORIAL TECHNIQUES AND COMBAT STYLES"

New recruits would have to master the pilum (javelin) and the gladius (sword), as well as battlefield formations

Backbreaking work, relentless training and routine marches

Washing
Soldiers were expected to maintain their own equipment but also their own personal hygiene during their limited free time each day. While barracks often had comfortable adjoining bathhouses, when on campaign troops would wash with whatever resources they could find.

Training
Soldiers were expected to train daily, practising for real combat with wooden swords, slings, bows and javelins. Repeating tough battlefield drills prepared soldiers mentally and physically to face the enemy for real.

Martial punishment
Discipline was essential in the army, and breaking any rules could earn a severe sentence. Theft, desertion, disobeying orders and other crimes were often punishable by demotion, beatings, flogging or even public execution by clubbing.

Building fortifications
All soldiers would help with the construction of a new temporary fortification at the end of each day's march, building trenches and wooden walls around the camp. This meant that no matter where the army travelled, it could ensure some level of protection from enemy attacks at night.

Marching
An army would be regularly ordered to march up to nine hours per day, with each soldier carrying their equipment and rations, which could weigh up to 40 kilograms (88 pounds). Disciplined marching was often the first thing taught to new recruits.

While auxiliaries were generally paid a little less than legionaries, they had the additional lure of being granted full Roman citizenship on completion of 25 years' military service.

Anyone looking to earn a little more could seek out both wealth and glory in war. In the aftermath of a battle, generals were known to reward particularly brave actions, or those who had received grisly wounds in the line of duty. After the Battle of Dyrrhachium (48 BCE), for example, Julius Caesar was presented with a shield that had been pierced by over a hundred arrows – he rewarded its owner, a centurion, with riches and honourable promotion.

However, during campaigns men often found less honourable ways to gain wealth. After a successful conquest, generals would often allow their men to pillage and loot, enabling them to fill their pockets with the spoils of war. In many extreme cases, generals used this as a way to secure the loyalty of the army and prevent possible mutinies in the ranks. Legionaries lucky to live long enough could receive a bonus of 12,000 sesterces (praemia) upon retiring or even be granted land to settle down, often within the same region in which they served.

STRUCTURE OF THE ARMY

Legions were highly organised fighting forces, with rigid command structures

PRAEFECTUS CASTRORUM
The third most senior officer in the army, the 'camp prefect' oversaw the maintenance of all arms, armour, fortifications and camp logistics.

KEY

Legionary   Centurion   Trumpeter

Praefectus castrorum   Equites   Aquilifer   Legatus legionis   Optio

Tribunus angusticlavius   Signifer   Tribunus laticlavius

DECLINE OF THE LEGIONS

Towards the middle of the 4th century CE, the Roman Empire was past the height of its power, and several fearsome tribes – Goths, Vandals, Huns and others – began threatening its borders. Armies garrisoned at the furthest edges of imperial territory, such as in Britain, were marched back down the roads to defend Roman heartlands. By this period the legions had dramatically changed from the dominating forces of previous centuries.

Original height and age requirements were overlooked as recruiters struggled to fill the ranks to defend the empire. There was also little time for the strict training regimes of previous eras, and the wisdom of the armatura was all but forgotten. Without the allure of sharing in the riches of conquests, men were often forced into service rather than volunteering.

COHORTS
A legion was made up of ten cohorts, each containing six centuries. Each century was comprised of 80 soldiers.

By this time, non-citizens were no longer prevented from becoming legionaries, while Roman citizens were also as likely to join auxiliary units. This meant that Rome's armies were no longer filled with men from the regions close to Rome itself but from among so-called 'barbarian' territories conquered by the empire, some even from beyond its borders. Although these new legions did achieve some victories, they paled in comparison to the elite fighting forces they once were.

TRIBUNUS LATICLAVIUS
The second in command of the army was a senior tribune appointed by the Senate or the emperor and identified by a broad stripe in his uniform.

AQUILIFER
A prestigious position, the 'eagle-bearer' had the honour of carrying the legion's standard into battle. He was also responsible for soldiers' pay.

EQUES LEGIONIS
Each legion also included a 120-man-strong cavalry unit.

AUXILIARIES

Although heavy infantry formed the backbone of Roman armies, specialist troops such as archers, slingers and cavalrymen were also crucial on the battlefield. These units were largely recruited from conquered territories, such as Gaul, Greece, Germania and Britain. Archers from Crete, for instance, were renowned for their skill with the bow, while German cavalrymen proved to be instrumental during Julius Caesar's conquest of the Gauls in 58–50 BCE.

While auxiliary units were often raised and disbanded to meet the needs of a legion, the Romans became increasingly reliant on them. Unlike their legionary comrades, these men were not considered Roman citizens, but citizenship could be earned through lengthy service. As the empire began to decline, auxiliary and legionary units became almost indistinguishable. Eventually, non-citizens were widely recruited to help defend Roman territory.

A depiction of an auxiliary infantryman from Rome's imperial period

TRIBUNUS ANGUSTICLAVII
Five tribunes, identified by a narrow stripe on their uniform, were responsible for the army's administration, but they occasionally led cohorts.

CENTURION
The commander of a centuria, usually promoted through the ranks, would have many years' experience. The most senior centurion in each legion was called the primus pili, or 'first spear'.

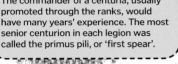

Century structure

Legionaries

Optio (assistant centurion)

Centurion

Signifer

Trumpeter

LEGATUS LEGIONIS
The overall commander of the legion, the legionary legate was usually a former politician, appointed directly by the emperor or Senate.

Below: A reenactment shows a centuria on the march, led by a centurion, signifiers and a trumpeter

GALEA
Made of bronze, the helmet protected against attacks to the head, neck and face.

PILUM
Measuring up to two metres (six feet seven inches) long, the metal barb of these javelins was designed to bend upon impact.

GLADIUS
These short iron blades were the primary weapon for Rome's infantry, designed for thrusting and stabbing.

SCUTUM
These large, rectangular shields protected much of the body from the neck down.

ROMAN LEGION RECRUITMENT REQUIREMENTS

1 Citizenship
Only a citizen of Rome could become a legionary. Freed or current slaves couldn't join, although this rule was relaxed as the needs of the army changed.

2 Height
Recruits were expected to be a minimum height of 1.72 metres (five feet eight inches), though for some roles even taller men were required.

3 Age
Boys as young as 17 could join the ranks, and men generally aged anywhere up to their mid-20s would be accepted. In desperate times, this maximum age was extended to 35.

4 Education
Although the ordinary soldier did not need any education, those wishing to gain officer posts needed basic numeracy and literacy skills.

5 Strength
Most important was the recruit's health, stamina, eyesight and strength. Soldiers incapable of carrying out the highly physical tasks demanded of them were often discharged from the army.

ARMS AND ARMOUR
Roman soldiers were equipped with the best weapons and protection of the period

Illustrations • Ed Crookes & Ian Jackson

ANCIENT GREEK THEATRE

UNCOVER THE CIVILISATION THAT INVENTED THE PLAY AND SET THE STAGE FOR WESTERN CULTURE

We have a lot to thank Ancient Greece for. From democracy to philosophy, this thriving collection of city-states was the birthplace of so many things that we take for granted today – including theatre.

The first mention of it dates back to 532 BCE, when an actor called Thespis performed a tragedy. His name has been immortalised as a term for a performer – a 'thespian'. A few decades later, a festival called the City Dionysia was established in Athens to honour Dionysus, the god of wine.

The events centred on competitive performances of tragedies and, from 487 BCE, comedies. Thousands flocked from all over Greece, businesses closed and prisoners were released to take part in five days of festivities.

Performances were staged at the Theatre of Dionysus, considered by many to be the first ever built. This was a huge open-air arena that could seat up to 17,000 people on rows of benches set into a hill. The actors performed in the centre, known as the orchestra, while a backdrop was painted onto a building behind the stage that was known as the skene. This was also where the actors changed into their masks and costumes.

The theatre's acoustics were so well thought out that every single audience member would have been able to hear the actors performing, even in the days before microphones and sound systems. Over 2,000 years later, we are still basing our theatre designs on these incredible ancient structures.

The ruins of the Theatre of Dionysus as they appear today

HOW TO PUT ON A PLAY IN ANCIENT GREECE
Follow these steps to produce your very own dramatic masterpiece

1 Pick a genre
In Ancient Greece, tragedy and comedy should never mix. The City Dionysia pits the writers of these two genres against each other in its annual theatre competition, so choose a side and get planning.

2 Get funding
Plays in Athens are publicly funded, but you will need to pitch your idea to an official, who is known as the eponymous archon, and get his approval, before you see the colour of his money.

3 Decide your actors
The eponymous archon is responsible for deciding your lead actors, which is done by drawing random lots. The chorus actors are paid for by wealthy citizens looking to win public favour.

4 Start writing
Not only do your plays have to be written in verse, but you'll also need to compose the music to accompany them. As for subject matter, the more revolutionary the better.

5 Perform your play
Once rehearsals are over, it's finally time to bring your work to the stage. The competitions can attract up to 17,000 audience members, and they last from dawn until dusk.

6 Collect your prize
The judges write their scores on tablets and place them in urns. The eponymous archon draws five of them at random and the winner is awarded with a wreath and a goat!

Illustrations • Edward Crooks

POMPEII CASTS

DISCOVER HOW THE VICTIMS OF A VOLCANIC ERUPTION HAVE BEEN PRESERVED

The famous preserved Pompeii 'bodies' are actually plaster casts of the cavities left by the victims

On 24 August 79 CE, Italy's Mount Vesuvius erupted with a violent explosion of lava, rock and ash, sending a cloud of debris 32 kilometres (20 miles) into the air. The nearby town of Herculaneum was soon hit with a scolding pyroclastic surge of volcanic materials, instantly incinerating everyone in its path, while ash and pumice rained down on the neighbouring city of Pompeii.

Some residents managed to flee in terror, but others stayed in their homes, hoping the danger would pass. The next morning, a second pyroclastic surge ploughed into the city, suffocating those that remained with toxic volcanic gas and burying them in mud and ash.

Pompeii was lost for 1,500 years before it was rediscovered in 1599, and after another 150 years a wide-scale excavation of the city began. As archaeologists were digging through the debris, they noticed distinct cavities, some of which contained human bones. They soon realised that these were perfect moulds of the dead, left behind after their bodies had decomposed.

At first they couldn't work out how to preserve the cavities, but following his appointment as

> ## "POMPEII WAS LOST FOR 1,500 YEARS BEFORE IT WAS REDISCOVERED"

director of the excavations in 1863, Giuseppe Fiorelli came up with an ingenious solution. He poured plaster into them so that it would set to form exact replicas of the victims at the moment of their death. It was a difficult process, as the plaster had to be mixed to exactly the right consistency so that it was thick enough to support the skeleton but not so thick that it destroyed the fine details of the mould. When they chipped away at the surrounding rock and revealed the final casts, some showed intricate details of hairstyles, clothing and faces.

Of the 1,150 bodies discovered at Pompeii, around 100 have been preserved in this way, providing a unique insight into their lives and deaths. Today, techniques like 3D scanning have even enabled scientists to create digital images of what the victims actually looked like, truly bringing them back to life almost 2,000 years after they met their cruel fate.

RESTORING THE DEAD

Discover how archaeologists created lifelike casts of Vesuvius' victims

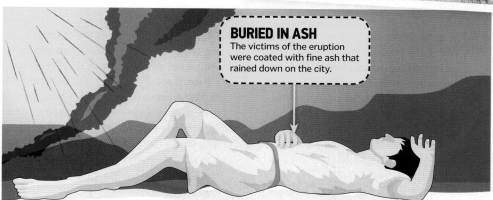

BURIED IN ASH
The victims of the eruption were coated with fine ash that rained down on the city.

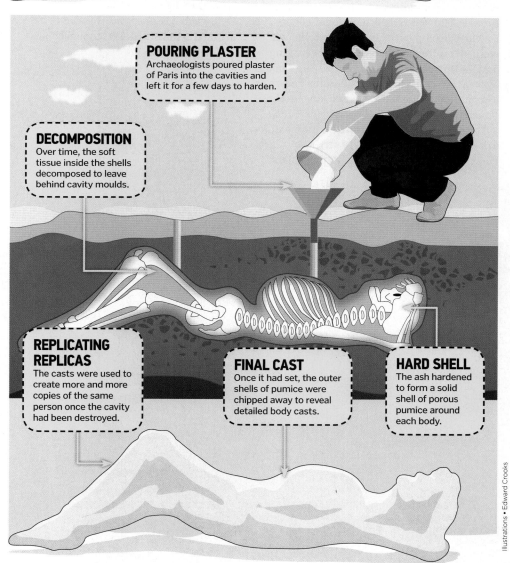

POURING PLASTER
Archaeologists poured plaster of Paris into the cavities and left it for a few days to harden.

DECOMPOSITION
Over time, the soft tissue inside the shells decomposed to leave behind cavity moulds.

REPLICATING REPLICAS
The casts were used to create more and more copies of the same person once the cavity had been destroyed.

FINAL CAST
Once it had set, the outer shells of pumice were chipped away to reveal detailed body casts.

HARD SHELL
The ash hardened to form a solid shell of porous pumice around each body.

Illustrations • Edward Crooks

THE MAUSOLEUM AT HALICARNASSUS

THE ANCIENT TOMB THAT WAS REDISCOVERED BETWEEN THE BRICKS OF A CASTLE

One of the Seven Wonders of the Ancient World, the Mausoleum at Halicarnassus was once the resting place of the king of Caria, a province in the Persian Empire (now Bodrum, Turkey) with Halicarnassus as its capital. Mausolus ruled over the region from around 377 BCE until his death in 353 BCE, after which his wife, Artemisia II, commissioned the construction of what would become their joint tomb.

Greek architects Satyros and Pythius designed the building, while leading sculptors Bryaxis, Timotheus, Leochares and Scopas provided decoration. Hundreds of craftsmen worked together to create a tomb fit for a king, and the finished monumental structure stood at over 42 metres (137 feet) tall. It became known as a 'mausoleum' after the deceased king in whose honour it was built.

The mausoleum stood in all of its grandeur for around 16 centuries, but then a series of earthquakes destroyed its supportive pillars, bringing the roof crashing to the ground. By 1404, the towering tomb had been reduced to nothing but its square base, which was covered with stone ruins. However, the fallen stones would still prove useful. In 1522, rumours of a Turkish invasion descended upon Bodrum: the fallen marble from the mausoleum was used to reinforce and fortify Bodrum Castle's walls, and some sculptures were also ground up to form lime for plaster.

Remnants of the once towering tomb can still be seen in between the bricks of Bodrum Castle. Other statues and excavated artefacts are held at the British Museum in London.

Main Image Source • Getty

REDISCOVERING AN ANCIENT RELIC

Sir Charles Thomas Newton, a 19th-century British archaeologist, was the first to unearth the remains of the once giant mausoleum around 1856. He noticed that some of the decorations on Bodrum Castle bore a resemblance to those thought to be on the mausoleum, and so the hunt began.

By studying works by writers of the time, Newton was able to pinpoint the location where it would have stood, which we now know to be Bodrum in Turkey. After purchasing the potential plot of land for the mausoleum, Newton excavated tunnels to surrounding areas and discovered stairs, walls and corners belonging to the legendary structure. Further excavations led to the discovery of sculpture remains, including the wheel from the roof chariot and the statues of both Mausolus and Artemisia, confirming the site's ancient past.

Ruins of the once towering tomb can still be seen in modern-day Bodrum

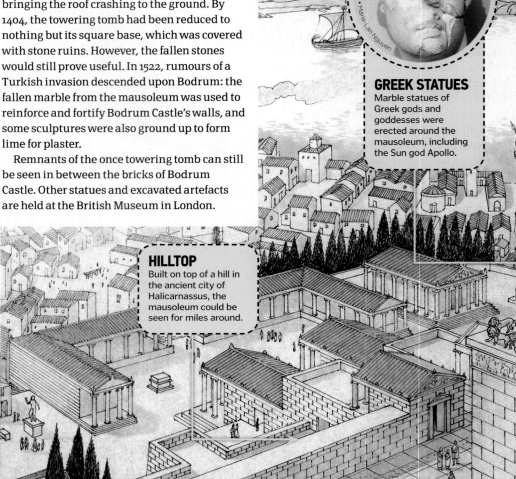

BREAKING DOWN THE MAUSOLEUM

How would this highly decorated piece of architecture have looked during its prime?

Image • Marie-Lan Nguyen

GREEK STATUES
Marble statues of Greek gods and goddesses were erected around the mausoleum, including the Sun god Apollo.

HILLTOP
Built on top of a hill in the ancient city of Halicarnassus, the mausoleum could be seen for miles around.

Image Source • Following Hadrian

AN ANCIENT GIANT
The entire structure of the mausoleum reached above 42 metres (137 feet) and was surrounded by a courtyard with warrior statues stationed at each corner.

MARBLE MAUSOLUS
Stood at the top of the mausoleum were huge marble statues of Mausolus and Artemisia riding in a four-horse-drawn chariot (quadriga).

Image • Carole Raddato

PILLARS
36 stone columns made up the mid section of the mausoleum, which also supported the 24-step pyramidal roof.

CARVINGS
At the base of the mausoleum, the stone was decorated with relief sculptures depicting different battle scenes between the Greeks and Amazons.

Image • Carole Raddato

Queen Artemisia II was also a botanist – the plant genus Artemisia is named after her

THE OTHER WORLD WONDERS

1 Great Pyramid of Giza
The oldest and only remaining intact ancient wonder, the Pyramid of Khufu was built some 4,500 years ago.

2 Hanging Gardens of Babylon
Constructed under the orders of the Babylonian king Nebuchadnezzar II around 600 BCE, the gardens sat near the Euphrates River in what is now the city of Hillah in central Iraq.

3 Statue of Zeus at Olympia
Created by Greek sculptor Phidias around 430 BCE, this 12-metre-tall statue was plated with gold and ivory and resided in the Temple of Zeus.

4 Temple of Artemis at Ephesus
Constructed around the mid 6th century in what is now Turkey, this building was a place of worship to Artemis, the Greek goddess of the hunt.

5 Colossus of Rhodes
Erected around 280 BCE, the bronze figure of the Greek god Helios stood around 30 metres (98 feet) tall until an earthquake brought him to his knees just 60 years later.

6 Lighthouse of Alexandria
Designed by Greek architect Sostratos around 270 BCE and said to be some 115 metres (377 feet) tall, this majestic tower sat on a small island called Pharos near the harbour of Alexandria.

Image • Marie-Lan Nguyen

THE AFTERLIFE IN ANCIENT EGYPT

EXPLORE THE RITUALS, DEMONS AND GODS OF THE UNDERWORLD

Image Source • Joe Cummings

Few cultures conjure as much intrigue and horror as that of the Ancient Egyptians. The civilisation that sprung up along the banks of the Nile around 3000 BCE was among the most powerful on Earth. Though much of Egypt was an uninhabitable desert wasteland, the river was a life source that nourished soil and watered crops.

It gave birth to a society of farmers, doctors, builders and soldiers, whose achievements and inventions were greater than any seen before. They created one of the first writing systems, were among the first to practise science, and their art was a blueprint for the Renaissance masters. But the achievements that the Ancient Egyptians are best remembered for are their towering pyramids and gory mummification rituals. Death was an industry, and a booming one at that.

Religion was the pillar upon which this society was built, and it guided every aspect of life. They believed that there were many gods, each of which had a different role – from Sekhmet, the goddess of war, to Hapi, the god of the Nile, who brought the floods every year. But perhaps the most important element of the Ancient Egyptian religion was the belief in the afterlife. When a person died, it was thought that their soul could live on, but only if it successfully navigated the underworld. First it would have to battle demons and gatekeepers, before arriving at the Hall of Judgement where it would have to prove itself worthy of eternal peace. Those who passed the test could proceed to the Field of Rushes – a heavenly reflection of life on Earth. Those who failed would be forever restless, stuck in a purgatory that was worse than death itself.

Because of these beliefs, the Ancient Egyptians spent their whole lives preparing for their journey through the underworld. Not only did this mean avoiding sin as much as possible, but it also meant ensuring that their physical being had somewhere to rest, and it was accompanied by all of the things their spirit would need to thrive in the afterlife. Wealthy Egyptians spent years building tombs that were often more elaborate than their own homes, and filling them with priceless treasures. In Ancient Egypt, death really was an awfully big adventure.

> "WEALTHY EGYPTIANS SPENT YEARS BUILDING TOMBS MORE ELABORATE THAN THEIR OWN HOMES"

PYRAMIDS AND TOMBS

In the early days of Ancient Egypt, pharaohs and other wealthy members of society were buried in mastabas. These were flat-roofed, rectangular structures with sloping sides, which helped to protect the grave from scavenging animals and thieves. But during the Third Dynasty, an architect named Imhotep came up with the idea of stacking multiple mastabas on top of each other, creating a much taller structure composed of a number of 'steps'. This would act as a staircase, allowing the deceased to ascend to the heavens. The first was called the Pyramid of Djoser, and it was built around 2680 BCE.

Over the next few hundred years, pyramids became the norm for pharaonic burials, and eventually the sides became smooth rather than stepped. Kings and queens competed to build the tallest, most magnificent monuments, but this came at a cost – huge amounts of stone were needed to build them, not to mention the costs of labour. Pyramids were also easy targets for gravediggers. By the time of the Seventh Dynasty, it was much more common for pharaohs to be buried in tombs carved deep into the rock.

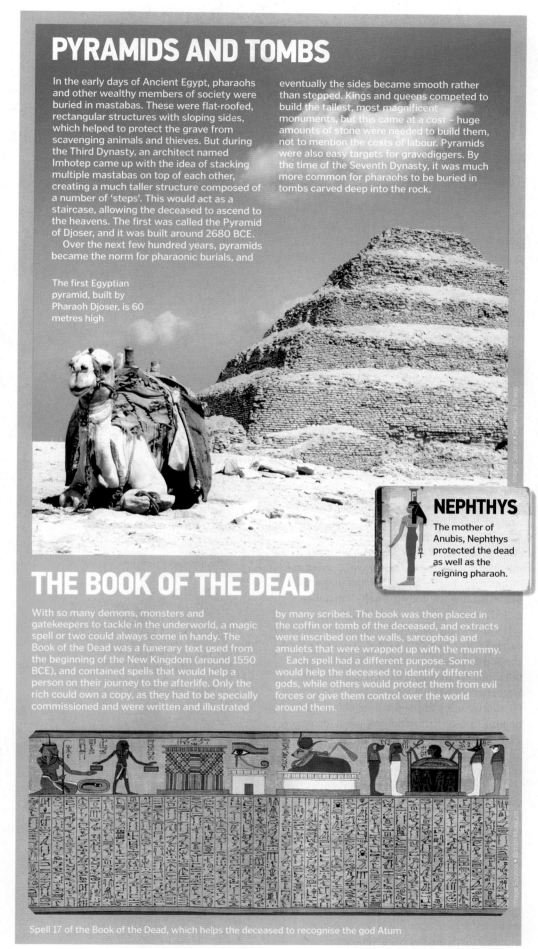

The first Egyptian pyramid, built by Pharaoh Djoser, is 60 metres high

NEPHTHYS
The mother of Anubis, Nephthys protected the dead as well as the reigning pharaoh.

THE BOOK OF THE DEAD

With so many demons, monsters and gatekeepers to tackle in the underworld, a magic spell or two could always come in handy. The Book of the Dead was a funerary text used from the beginning of the New Kingdom (around 1550 BCE), and contained spells that would help a person on their journey to the afterlife. Only the rich could own a copy, as they had to be specially commissioned and were written and illustrated by many scribes. The book was then placed in the coffin or tomb of the deceased, and extracts were inscribed on the walls, sarcophagi and amulets that were wrapped up with the mummy.

Each spell had a different purpose. Some would help the deceased to identify different gods, while others would protect them from evil forces or give them control over the world around them.

Spell 17 of the Book of the Dead, which helps the deceased to recognise the god Atum

MAKING A MUMMY

THE EMBALMING PROCESS WAS LONG AND GRUESOME

The key to eternal life wasn't just preserving the soul – Ancient Egyptians believed it had to return to its body regularly in order to survive, so that too would need to be kept intact. They also believed that the deceased must resemble the living as much as possible in order for the spirit to recognise its physical home. Initially, this was achieved by burying the dead in the desert, where the hot sand would dehydrate bodies and delay decomposition. But over time, the Egyptians developed an artificial method of preservation that would enable their remains to last for millennia: mummification.

The first mummies date back to 2600 BCE, but it wasn't until around 1550 BCE that the most effective and well-known mummification method was developed. This involved removing the internal organs, dehydrating the flesh, and then wrapping the entire body in linen bandages. The process took around 70 days and was extremely costly, so only the very rich could afford it. Poorer families were treated with another method of embalmment, which involved liquidising the organs with cedar tree oil and draining them out through the rectum, before placing the body in a salty substance called natron that would help dry it out.

Because of the climate, embalmment was carried out as soon as possible after death. First the body was taken to an ibu, or place of purification – usually a tent close to the Nile. Here it would be purified using water and palm oil, representing the deceased's rebirth, and helping to keep them smelling sweet for longer. Then the body was taken to the per nefer, another tent where the embalmment would take place.

Only priests were qualified to carry out this procedure, with the chief embalmer known as the 'hery seshta'. This man represented Anubis, the god of embalming and the dead, and often wore a jackal mask to show his importance. He was responsible for wrapping the body and performing religious rites over the deceased – an element of the process just as vital as the preservation of the body. Thanks to this process, we can now gaze upon the faces of people almost exactly as they were 3,000 years ago.

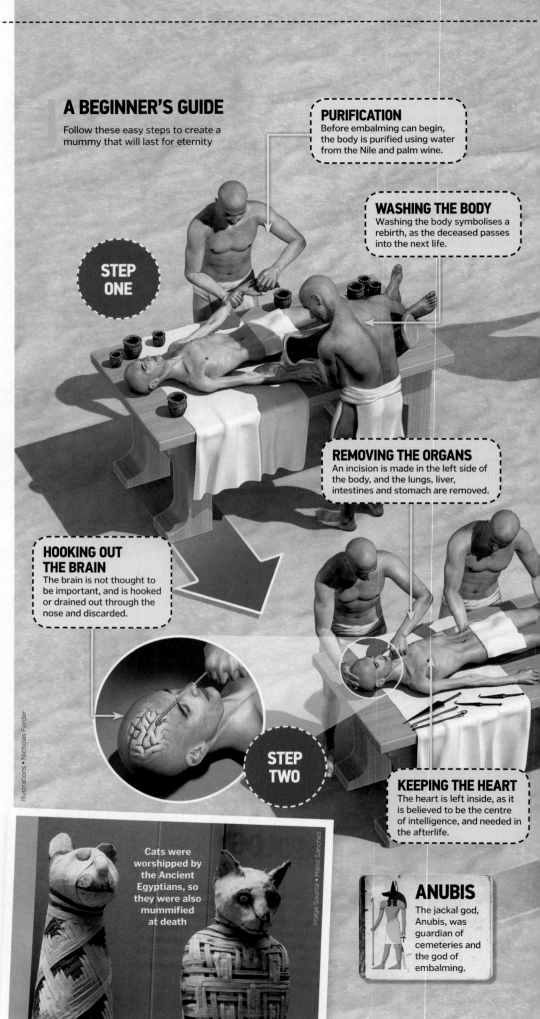

A BEGINNER'S GUIDE

Follow these easy steps to create a mummy that will last for eternity

PURIFICATION
Before embalming can begin, the body is purified using water from the Nile and palm wine.

WASHING THE BODY
Washing the body symbolises a rebirth, as the deceased passes into the next life.

STEP ONE

REMOVING THE ORGANS
An incision is made in the left side of the body, and the lungs, liver, intestines and stomach are removed.

HOOKING OUT THE BRAIN
The brain is not thought to be important, and is hooked or drained out through the nose and discarded.

STEP TWO

KEEPING THE HEART
The heart is left inside, as it is believed to be the centre of intelligence, and needed in the afterlife.

Illustrations • Nicholas Forder

Cats were worshipped by the Ancient Egyptians, so they were also mummified at death

Image Source • Mario Sánchez

ANUBIS
The jackal god, Anubis, was guardian of cemeteries and the god of embalming.

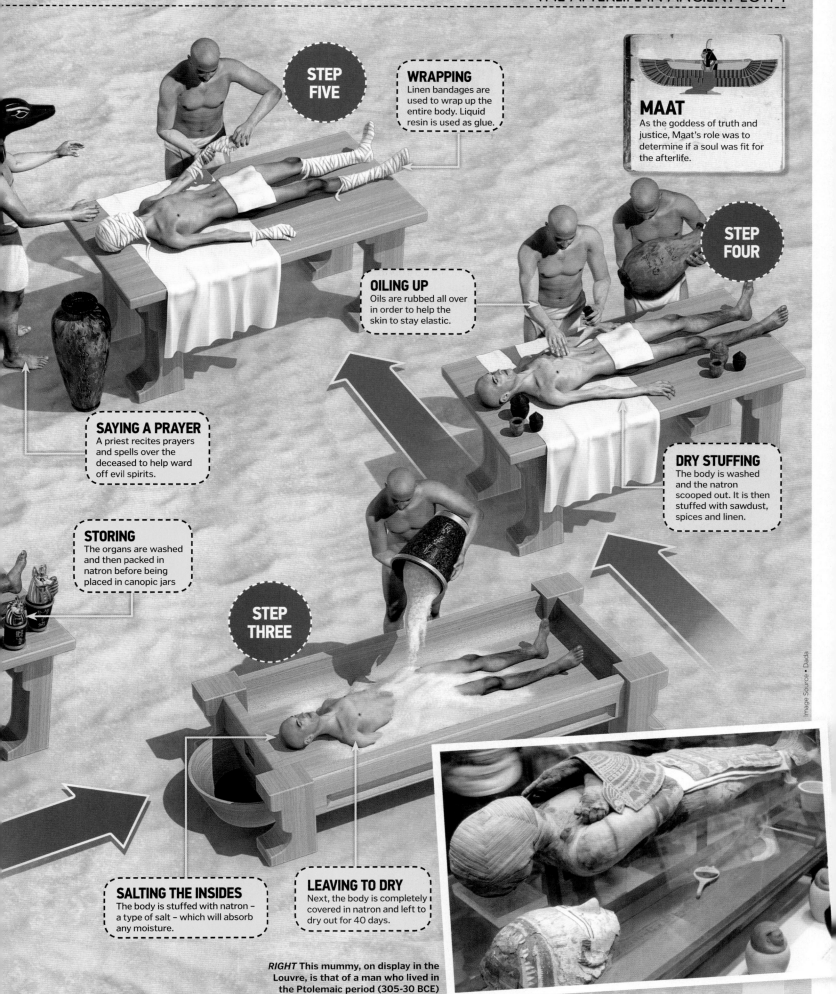

STEP FIVE

WRAPPING
Linen bandages are used to wrap up the entire body. Liquid resin is used as glue.

MAAT
As the goddess of truth and justice, Maat's role was to determine if a soul was fit for the afterlife.

STEP FOUR

OILING UP
Oils are rubbed all over in order to help the skin to stay elastic.

SAYING A PRAYER
A priest recites prayers and spells over the deceased to help ward off evil spirits.

DRY STUFFING
The body is washed and the natron scooped out. It is then stuffed with sawdust, spices and linen.

STORING
The organs are washed and then packed in natron before being placed in canopic jars

STEP THREE

SALTING THE INSIDES
The body is stuffed with natron – a type of salt – which will absorb any moisture.

LEAVING TO DRY
Next, the body is completely covered in natron and left to dry out for 40 days.

RIGHT This mummy, on display in the Louvre, is that of a man who lived in the Ptolemaic period (305-30 BCE)

Image Source • Dada

47

FUNERALS AND BURIAL

EGYPTIANS DEPARTED THIS WORLD WITH ALL THEIR HOME COMFORTS

ISIS
Along with her sister, Nepthys, Isis protected the dead, and was goddess of children.

OSIRIS
Osiris, depicted as a mummified pharaoh, was god of the afterlife.

Long before their deaths, wealthy Egyptians would build their tombs and pile them high with things they would need in the afterlife. From tables and chairs to chariots, jewellery and mummified pets, they could guarantee that their spirit would never want for anything.

Food was just as important in the afterlife as it had been in their worldly one, so copious amounts of wine, fruit and grains were also buried with the dead. Even meat was included, which was often salted or even mummified to prevent it from rotting. If the worst came to the worst, they could always paint food on the walls – the Ancient Egyptians believed that in the land of the dead, depictions were just as edible as the physical products.

Also placed in the tomb were shabtis. These were small figurines, often made from clay, wood or stone, which would act as servants in the afterlife. Some people were buried with just one or two, whereas others – like Pharaoh Taharqa – were buried with over 1,000.

Poorer Egyptians had less elaborate tombs, while those at the very bottom of society were simply wrapped in cloth and buried in the desert with everyday objects like pots and perhaps a weapon of some kind. But everyone, rich or poor, was given a ceremony, as this was considered necessary in order for his or her spirit to pass to the underworld.

Wealthy Egyptians were given an elaborate funeral, during which the body of the dead was carried to the tomb accompanied by a procession of mourners and dancers. Two women called 'kites' were also present, whose job it was to mourn overtly. According to Ancient Egyptian religion, the greater a showing of grief, the better the soul would fare in the Hall of Judgement.

At the tomb, a priest performed the 'Opening of the Mouth' ceremony, in which the mummy was propped upright and a ceremonial blade pressed against the mouth. This would enable them to breathe, talk and eat in the afterlife. The action was repeated on the eyes and limbs to allow the spirit to see and move. The coffin was placed in a sarcophagus, offerings left, prayers recited and the tomb sealed.

A FUNERAL FIT FOR A PHARAOH
These elaborate send-offs prepared the body for the lands of the living and the dead

DEATH MASK
A funerary mask resembling the deceased ensures that the spirit will be able to recognise its body.

FUNERAL PROCESSION
A procession of mourners carries the coffin and grave goods to the tomb. Some of the mourners are paid to weep loudly throughout.

INTO THE COFFIN
A painted 'cartonnage' case is attached to the mummy, then it is placed in a 'suhet' (coffin).

OPENING OF THE MOUTH
At the tomb, a priest performs the Opening of the Mouth ceremony, so the deceased can breathe and speak in the afterlife.

SARCOPHOGUS
The coffin is placed in a sarcophagus – an alabaster box designed to provide extra protection.

SEALED WITH A SPELL
Both the sarcophagus and tomb are sealed before the priest casts a spell to protect them, known as the Curse of the Pharaohs.

Image Source • Getty

TUTANKHAMUN'S METEORITE DAGGER

In June 2016, researchers announced that a dagger found by Howard Carter in the tomb of Tutankhamun appeared to be made with iron from a meteorite. The blade had puzzled archaeologists for decades, as ironwork was rare in Ancient Egypt and the metal had not rusted. An X-ray fluorescence spectrometer was used to discover its chemical composition. The high nickel content, as well as the presence of cobalt "strongly suggests an extra-terrestrial origin", and similar levels have in fact been found in a meteorite that crashed 240 kilometres (149 miles) west of Alexandria before or during the time of Tutankhamun.

The iron blade (right) is believed to be made from a meteorite

Image Source • Alamy

ANUBIS
The god of embalming attended the ceremony and ushered successful souls into the afterlife.

BALANCING THE SCALES
If the heart balanced against the feather, the soul of the deceased could continue to the afterlife.

OSIRIS
The ceremony took place before Osiris, god of the dead and the afterlife, and a tribunal of 42 deities.

HEART
If the heart was heavy with the weight of wrongdoings, it was devoured by the crocodile demoness, Amuut.

FEATHER OF TRUTH
The heart was weighed against the feather of the goddess Maat, which represented truth and justice.

JOURNEY TO THE AFTERLIFE
SECURING A PLACE IN THE HEAVENS WAS EASIER SAID THAN DONE

No amount of money spent on tombs or time spent memorising spells could guarantee an Ancient Egyptian a place in the afterlife. First, their soul would have to conquer the obstacles and demons of the underworld, and then face the judgement of the gods in the Weighing of the Heart ceremony. Only the worthiest souls could proceed to the Field of Rushes, where they would exist in pleasure for eternity.

The Ancient Egyptians believed that when a person was buried, their spirit departed their body and descended to the underworld (Duat). There, it must pass through 12 gates, each of which was guarded by a different deity, which the spirit must recognise and name. That may sound easy, but there were also monsters, demons and lakes of fire to contend with.

The Book of the Dead provided a list of spells that would help the spirit to overcome these obstacles. If successful, the soul would pass into the Hall of Judgement, where it would have to prove its worthiness in front of 42 deities. The Book of the Dead also helped the spirit with the right answers to their questions, so that it could

pass this stage of the test even without being entirely innocent.

Next, the spirit could proceed to the Weighing of the Heart ceremony. This was overseen by Osiris, the chief god of the underworld. The Egyptians believed the heart contained a record of all of the deceased's actions in life, so it was weighed against the feather of the goddess Maat to determine how virtuous they had been. If the scales balanced, the spirit was welcomed into the afterlife by Osiris. If the heart was heavier than the feather, it was thrown to the crocodile demoness, Ammut, and the soul was cast into the darkness, condemned to an eternity of restlessness. Of course, the dead could always rely on their trusty book for help. A simple recital of spell 30B could help to prevent the heart from giving away their murky past.

Those lucky enough to secure a place in the afterlife would experience the magnificence of the Field of Rushes. The dead would be granted a plot of land on which to grow crops, assisted by the shabtis they had been buried with, and look forward to a future of eternal peace.

Egyptians were buried with all their worldly possessions, including beds and chariots

In the underworld, the spirit would have to battle giant serpents and other monsters

HAGIA SOPHIA

EXPLORE THE INNOVATIVE DESIGN AND RICH HISTORY OF TURKEY'S DOMED WONDER

Once a cathedral, then a mosque, and now a museum, the Hagia Sophia is an architectural jewel that has stood for 1,400 years. Its construction began in the 6th century CE, when Istanbul was known as Constantinople, the capital city of the Roman Byzantine Empire.

Its site had previously been home to the Magna Ecclesia, meaning 'Great Church' in Latin, which was burned down during riots in 404 CE, and then another church, which was destroyed during the Nika Revolt in 532 CE. At that time, Emperor Justinian I was the ruler of the empire, and once the revolt against him had been suppressed, he ordered a grand new cathedral to be built. He commissioned Anthemius of Tralles, a mathematician and physicist, and Elder Isidore of Miletus, a professor of geometry and mechanics, to lead the project, and although neither had much architectural experience, they managed to design a domed structure that was incredibly innovative for its time. Less than six years later, construction of the world's largest cathedral was complete, a title it retained until the Seville Cathedral surpassed it 1,000 years later.

By the time the Byzantine Empire ended in 1453, the Hagia Sophia had fallen into disrepair, but when Mehmed II, the Sultan of the new Ottoman Empire, saw it he was greatly impressed. He decided to turn it into the grand mosque of the sultans, and so a library, a fountain, a kitchen to feed the poor, and towers, called minarets, at each corner were later built.

Almost 500 years later, the building's purpose changed yet again when the first Turkish president came into power. He ordered for the Hagia Sophia to be turned into a museum, and in 1935 it opened its doors to the general public, allowing them to explore one of the greatest surviving examples of Byzantine architecture for themselves.

In 2020, Turkish President Recep Erdogan ordered that the Hagia Sophia be reconverted into a mosque.

BUTTRESSES
These structural supports were added by both Byzantine and Ottoman architects to help hold up the domed roof.

BENEATH THE DOME
An innovative design shaped by the Byzantine and Ottoman Empires

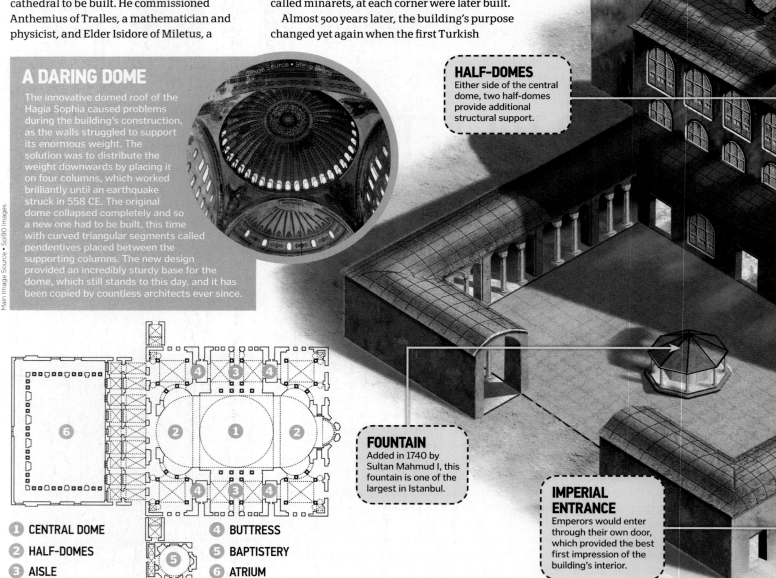

A DARING DOME
The innovative domed roof of the Hagia Sophia caused problems during the building's construction, as the walls struggled to support its enormous weight. The solution was to distribute the weight downwards by placing it on four columns, which worked brilliantly until an earthquake struck in 558 CE. The original dome collapsed completely and so a new one had to be built, this time with curved triangular segments called pendentives placed between the supporting columns. The new design provided an incredibly sturdy base for the dome, which still stands to this day, and it has been copied by countless architects ever since.

Main Image Source • Sol90 Images

Image Source • Steve Evans

HALF-DOMES
Either side of the central dome, two half-domes provide additional structural support.

FOUNTAIN
Added in 1740 by Sultan Mahmud I, this fountain is one of the largest in Istanbul.

IMPERIAL ENTRANCE
Emperors would enter through their own door, which provided the best first impression of the building's interior.

1. CENTRAL DOME
2. HALF-DOMES
3. AISLE
4. BUTTRESS
5. BAPTISTERY
6. ATRIUM

"THE DOMED STRUCTURE WAS INCREDIBLY INNOVATIVE FOR ITS TIME"

DOME
The dome is made of bricks and mortar, and measures 32 metres (105 feet) in diameter and sits 56 metres (183 feet) above the ground.

WINDOWS
40 arched windows around the base of the dome let in sunlight from all angles.

PENDENTIVES
These curved triangular segments join the dome's four supporting columns, providing a sturdy base.

APSE
The cathedral's alter was replaced with a mihrab pointing towards Mecca when it became a mosque.

AISLES
The two floors allowed visitors to be segregated by social class, with the upper gallery reserved for the emperor and his attendants.

ENTRANCE
Members of the public would enter through a side door and remain on the ground floor.

The name Hagia Sophia is Greek for 'holy wisdom'

Image Source •Arild Vågen

MASTERFUL MOSAICS

During its years as a Roman cathedral, the Hagia Sophia was decorated with ornate mosaics depicting emperors and religious figures, but not all of them can still be seen today. In 726 CE, Emperor Leo of Isaurian ordered religious mosaics to be destroyed, fearing the people would worship the images. His successors soon added more, but some were shipped to Venice in 1204, and the rest were covered with plaster and paint when the building became a mosque. However, since 1931, many of these works of art have been recovered and restored to their former glory.

Image Source • Myrabella derivative

The mosaic located above the imperial entrance dates back to the 9th or 10th century

THE MIDDLE AGES

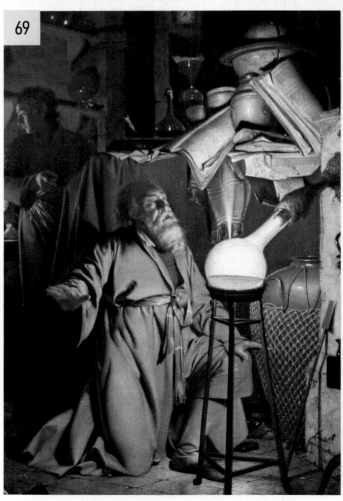

La Tour de PORCELAINE
PORCELLYNE TOOREN.

THE TERRIBLE TRUE STORIES OF THE TOWER OF LONDON

MURDERED CHILDREN, DECAPITATED QUEENS AND THE WORLD'S LARGEST DIAMOND – OVER 900 YEARS OF BRITAIN'S MOST FAMOUS FORTRESS

Words by **Jodie Tyley**

After his conquest of England in 1066, William of Normandy set about securing his throne by sending a clear message that he was here to stay – and it was a message written in stone. The king built castles all over the country to stamp his authority, and the biggest and most imposing of them all was London's White Tower.

To construct the Tower, William shipped stone over from Caen in France, while Anglo-Saxons provided most of the labour. It took around 20 years to complete and when it was finished it stood at 27 metres (89 feet) tall with walls 4.5 metres (15 feet) thick; walls designed to intimidate the defeated Londoners and act as a defence against them.

The second and third floors – the most secure parts of the keep – were reserved for royalty and nobles. This also includes St John's Chapel, one of the earliest Norman chapels in the country. The first floor was used by domestic staff, and the cellar stored provisions and wine racks. Years later it would house a different kind of rack – one designed for stretching limbs and breaking bones.

The original entrance was on the first floor. Now accessible via a wooden staircase, in Norman times this would have been a ladder that could be quickly withdrawn to prevent intruders. If enemies did gain access, the spiral staircase would have put them at a disadvantage. Right-handed attackers wouldn't have been able to swing their swords as effectively as the defenders – the wall would have got in the way. What's more, the steps vary in size, so anyone unfamiliar with the layout could lose their footing if they weren't careful, often fatal in a sword fight.

First and foremost, the Tower of London was a palace, not a prison. However, the first inmate was also the first escapee! Ranulf Flambard, Bishop of Durham, was imprisoned in 1100. A year later his friends smuggled in a rope inside a wine casket, which the guards heartily drank. As they slept, Ranulf is said to have used the rope to abseil to freedom.

> ## "FIRST AND FOREMOST, THE TOWER OF LONDON WAS A PALACE, NOT A PRISON"

The Tower of London continued as a royal residence for William the Conqueror's descendants, who made their own mark on the fortress. Henry III (1216-72) and his son Edward I (1272-1307) added royal apartments and built not one but two concentric walls of defence and a 50-metre- (164-foot-) wide moat – further than an archer could shoot accurately. However, in 1843 this moat was drained when sewage, carcasses and the bodies of plague victims turned it into a stinking pit of disease encircling the 2,500 people living in the Tower.

Another of the defensive features are the portcullises. French for 'sliding door', these heavy metal gates could be lowered and raised by a pulley. The most infamous of these lies at the bottom of St Thomas' Tower. Originally, this was used as the water-gate entrance for Edward I's royal barge. Later it became known as the

PROTECTING THE CROWN JEWELS

For over 600 years the Tower has housed precious royal items, but it was also where the original Crown Jewels were destroyed following the execution of King Charles I in 1649. Among the irreplaceable historical artefacts was the 11th-century crown of the saint-king Edward the Confessor, which was dropped into the Mint melting pot and turned into coins.

The Medieval coronation spoon was one of the few items that survived, and this 800-year-old object can be seen in the Tower's Jewel House today. This is also where the coronation regalia are displayed, created after the restoration of the monarchy in 1661. The most important item is the coronation crown itself, named St Edward's Crown in memory of its Medieval predecessor. This is only worn when a monarch is crowned, so for the past 65 years it has been unused.

These sacred and ceremonial objects were once stored over 80 metres (262 feet) below ground in a fortified bunker but were transferred upstairs in 1994. In their present, more accessible location in the Waterloo Barracks they are protected by bombproof display cases and over 100 hidden cameras. Massive vault doors with thick bolts secure entry into the room, and a control room where the security devices are located is strictly off-limits. The sentry, along with Yeoman Warders and the Jewel House wardens, also stand guard.

The Crown Jewels feature the Koh-i-Noor, the largest diamond in the world

Image Source • Joe Cummings

Image Source • Getty

trader's gate, where supplies were delivered, but then things took a dark turn. In the 16th century this same entrance became known as Traitors' Gate, and it was through here that prisoners were brought to the Tower to be tried. The route to the gate took the accused along the River Thames and under London Bridge, where the heads of executed prisoners gazed down at them from spikes.

In 1279, Edward I moved the Royal Mint to the Tower. This was where the coins of the realm were manufactured under the close scrutiny of guards. Medieval coins were made of silver, which was easy to bend and break, meaning criminals could flood the market with fake ones. When an enraged Edward learned of this ploy he placed the blame on England's small Jewish community, and many were consequently

hanged while 600 found themselves imprisoned in the Tower.

Bloody stories such as this earned the fortress a grisly reputation, and no one dared challenge its power until 1381 during the Peasants' Revolt. On 14 June that year, an angry mob of militant rebels breached the Tower walls. One of their targets, the archbishop of Canterbury and the king's chancellor, was saying his last prayers in the chapel when

they seized him. He was dragged to Tower Hill and promptly beheaded.

Clearly being a resident of the castle did not always guarantee your safety. During the Wars of the Roses, Henry VI was murdered while at

A TOUR OF THE TOWER
The medieval castle has served many purposes over the centuries

CHAPEL ROYAL OF ST PETER AD VINCULA
There has been a place of worship on this site for over 1,000 years. However, the chapel that stands today dates from the reign of Henry VIII (1509-47).

TOWER GREEN
Only high-ranking prisoners were beheaded inside the Tower. Seven nobles were executed on Tower Green, including two wives of Henry VIII.

WAKEFIELD TOWER
These were the royal lodgings of Henry III (Edward I's father). They were originally on the river's edge so that he could arrive by boat.

QUEEN'S HOUSE
Henry VIII built these apartments for his second queen, Anne Boleyn. She stayed here before her coronation and again years later before her execution in 1536.

TRAITORS' GATE
The water gate was originally an entrance for Edward I to arrive by barge. It later became the entrance for prisoners condemned to the Tower.

ST THOMAS' TOWER
This was built by Edward I between 1275 and 1279 as royal accommodation with views of the river.

Main Image Source • Adrian Mann

TIMELINE OF THE TOWER

1070s
Following the Norman invasion in 1066, William the Conqueror began building the fortress to control the city of London.

1241
Henry III had the castle keep whitewashed. It then became known as the White Tower as a result.

1300s
The formal locking and unlocking of the Tower began on King Edward III's orders.

1381
The only time the Tower's defences failed was during the Peasants' Revolt when rebels ran through the gates.

1471
King Henry VI was murdered here during the Wars of the Roses. He was the last Lancastrian king.

1669
During the reign of Charles II, paying members of the public were permitted to visit the Tower.

1674
The remains of small children were discovered, believed to be the 'Princes in the Tower', who went missing in 1483.

1835
The Royal Menagerie was closed and the animals were moved to Regent's Park.

1952
Notorious East End gangsters the Kray twins were among the last prisoners to be held at the Tower.

1994
The Crown Jewels were moved up to the Jewel House, which was opened by Queen Elizabeth II.

WHITE TOWER
The foreboding castle keep was built by William the Conqueror between 1078 and 1097 to deter any would-be rebels and invaders.

WATERLOO BLOCK
As constable of the Tower, the Duke of Wellington ordered this block to be built in 1845 as barracks for some 1,000 men. It was named after his famous victory.

MARTIN TOWER
The former prison later housed the Crown Jewels from 1669 to 1841. It was here that Thomas Blood made an attempt to steal them.

THE FIRST LONDON ZOO

Long before humans were held captive in the Tower, wild beasts once paced the fortress. The Royal Menagerie was founded by King John in the early 1200s, as exotic creatures were seen as status symbols. His son, Henry III, honoured this strange tradition and the number of animals at the Tower grew. In 1235, Holy Roman Emperor Frederick II sent three lions, and in 1252 the king of Norway sent a polar bear.

The Royal Menagerie opened its doors to the public in the 18th century – the price of admission was three half-pence or a cat or dog that could be fed to the lions! However, at the beginning of the 19th century animal welfare became a priority and the RSPCA was founded. The Menagerie finally closed its doors and 150 animals were moved to Regent's Park, establishing London Zoo.

Fanny Howe, whelp'd in the Tower, 1794. Fanny was a female tiger housed in the Royal Menagerie

Image Source • Getty

Edward I's bedchamber has been re-created using replicas of 13th-century furnishings

Image Source • Alamy

LANTHORN TOWER
This tower was part of Henry III's queen's lodgings. It was also built to reinforce defences.

prayer in the King's Private Chapel in the Wakefield Tower. Years later, the children of his Yorkist enemy, Edward IV, mysteriously disappeared within the fortress.

It was 1483, and 12-year-old Edward V was awaiting his coronation. He was taken there, as was tradition, along with his nine-year-old brother. Better known as 'the Princes in the Tower', the boys became prisoners when their uncle Richard (who later became King Richard III) declared them illegitimate and took the crown for himself. Months later the princes vanished. Rumours of their murder saw the Garden Tower where they were kept renamed as the Bloody Tower. For centuries no one knew what happened, until renovation work in 1674 uncovered the skeletons of two children under a staircase in the White Tower.

Yet more royal blood would be spilled during the reign of King Henry VIII. This time, however, the executions were ordered by the state and carried out in full view of the public. The Tudor tyrant signed the death warrants of two of his wives, Anne Boleyn and Catherine Howard, and some of his closest friends, including Sir Thomas More. While most of these executions took place on the nearby Tower Hill, seven nobles were executed within the walls of the Tower in relative privacy.

A temporary wooden scaffold was erected on Tower Green – an open space by the Chapel Royal of St Peter ad Vincula – to give the onlookers a better view. The condemned would climb the stairs onto the platform and give the executioner a purse of gold and silver as a final act of forgiveness. They would then utter their last words before laying their head on the chopping block to await the blow of the executioner's axe.

In the case of Margaret Pole, Countess of Salisbury, it took several blows to finish the deed. The nobles who died here were buried in

Prisoners entered the Tower through Traitor's Gate

GUARDIANS OF THE TOWER

Yeoman Warders, nicknamed Beefeaters, have protected the fortress since Tudor times

TUDOR BONNET
Known as the Tudor bonnet, this large hat adds height to the wearer, making them appear more intimidating to any would-be attackers.

TUDOR STATE DRESS
The 'red and gilt' uniform has been worn since 1549 and was originally designed to be worn under armour. Today it is only worn when the monarch visits the Tower or during state occasions.

MEDALS
Today's Yeoman Warders must have completed at least 22 years' military service. They also need to have reached the rank of warrant officer and have been awarded the Long Service and Good Conduct Medal.

UNDRESS UNIFORM
This daily working uniform was granted to the Yeoman Warders by Queen Victoria in 1858. The frock coat features the initials of the current monarch.

KEYS
Every night, at precisely 9.53pm, the Chief Yeoman Warder, dressed in a red Tudor Watchcoat (not shown), locks the Tower gates. This ritual is known as the Ceremony of the Keys and it has been performed for the last 700 years.

BELT
The state dress is almost identical to the uniform of the Yeoman of the Guard – the bodyguards of the British monarch. However, the Warders wear a belt around their waist while the Guards wear cross-belts from the left shoulder.

EMBLEMS
The Tudor state dress has an embroidered thistle, rose and shamrock – the emblems of Scotland, England and Ireland. It was designed to be worn under armour, hence the tights.

Image Source • Getty

Image Source • Kevin Bradburn

the grounds, and a memorial stands on the scaffold site today.

The Tower had become Henry VIII's personal prison, and he believed it should be protected by part of the royal bodyguard. The Yeoman Warders were created in 1485 and have guarded the castle ever since. It is said that they gained the nickname of 'Beefeater' because they were originally paid in food, in particular beef as it was a luxury item. It was a coveted position and one that could be sold for 250 guineas until the duke of Wellington abolished this purchase system in 1826. In his role as Constable of the Tower he made other changes, such as getting rid of the Royal Menagerie, a collection of exotic animals that had been there since the 13th century. He wanted to keep the Tower as a strictly military stronghold and even built the Waterloo Barracks for 1,000 soldiers.

The Iron Duke didn't entirely get his wish though, as today the Tower of London is one of the most-visited tourist attractions in the world. It continues the tradition of housing the Crown Jewels, and Yeoman Warders still stand on ceremonial guard, but their duties now include giving guided tours. But the Tower doesn't shut down when the visitors leave. The 37 Warders live on the premises with their families, the Resident Governor and a garrison of soldiers. There's an onsite doctor and chaplain and even a secret pub. Over 900 years on, the castle that was built to inspire awe and fear in Londoners is now one of the city's most treasured landmarks.

The Beauchamp Tower bears the graffiti of prisoners from the 16th and 17th centuries

The 16th-century Queen's House overlooks the execution site of Tower Green

RAVEN MAD

Legend has it that if the Tower has fewer than six ravens in it, the fortress and kingdom will fall. That's why there are seven ravens in the Tower today – one extra just in case! There is even a Ravenmaster who looks after their wellbeing and keeps their feathers trimmed to prevent them from flying too far away.

It's said that Charles II ordered that the ravens were protected upon hearing the grim prophecy. This was much to the annoyance of astronomer John Flamsteed, who complained that the birds were hampering his work in the observatory in the White Tower.

The ravens have since become known as guardians of the Tower, but over the years some have gone absent without leave and others have been dismissed for bad behaviour.

The ravens are fed raw meat and biscuits soaked in blood

FAMOUS PRISONERS
MANY WELL-KNOWN PEOPLE SPENT TIME IN THE TOWER

ANNE BOLEYN
2 MAY 1536 – 19 MAY 1536

When Henry VIII's second queen did not give birth to a son she was arrested – and later executed – on trumped-up charges of treason, adultery and incest.

LADY JANE GREY
19 JULY 1553 – 12 FEBRUARY 1554

The 'Nine-Day Queen' was already at the Tower preparing for her coronation when her claim to power was overruled. She was imprisoned then executed.

GUY FAWKES
5 NOVEMBER 1605 – 31 JANUARY 1606

The head of the Gunpowder Plot was tortured in the Tower. Sentenced to be hung, drawn and quartered, he was spared this fate by breaking his neck.

SIR WALTER RALEIGH
1603 – 1616

Once the favourite of Elizabeth I, Raleigh was unpopular with her successor, James I. Accused of plotting against the king, he was imprisoned for 13 years before being executed.

THE PRINCES IN THE TOWER
JUNE 1483

Edward and Richard York were held in what became known as the Bloody Tower before they mysteriously disappeared after their uncle usurped the throne.

RUDOLF HESS
17–20 MAY 1941

Winston Churchill briefly imprisoned the Deputy Führer of Nazi Germany after Hess' plane crashed in Scotland. He claimed to have been travelling on a mission to broker peace.

Image Sources • Joe Cummings • National Portrait Gallery • John Everett Millais • German Federal Archives

MEDIEVAL JOBS

FROM CATCHING RATS IN SEWERS TO JUGGLING FOR THE KING, DISCOVER THE STRANGE CAREERS AVAILABLE IN THE MIDDLE AGES

The job opportunities open to you in Medieval times largely depended on your social class. Those with status were typically nobles, members of the clergy or employed by the royal court, while the peasants, or those without status, worked as craftsmen or labourers. In between were the merchants, who became wealthy by trading products that were made by skilled workers all over the world.

All roles were important, as they ensured that everyone had the goods and services they needed to go about their lives, but the lower-class workers often found themselves being exploited. As a result, the guild system was established. Guilds were organisations that promoted the economic welfare of their members, much like today's trade unions. Most professions had their own guilds, from merchants and weavers to blacksmiths and candlemakers. Members would set prices and standards for their trade; anyone seeking employment could pay to join and be trained in the represented craft.

HERBALIST

Using practical herbal remedies derived from plants and other natural sources, these so-called 'wise women' could treat a wide range of medical conditions. Providing a lifeline for those who could not afford the services of a trained physician, their knowledge of folk medicine was then passed down through the generations.

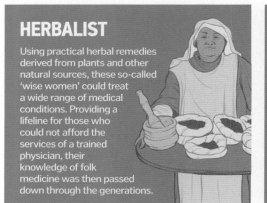

SQUIRE

Promoted from the position of page boy at 14, a squire was the servant to a knight, and often accompanied him into battle. In return, he would be taught the code of chivalry, the rules of heraldry, bravery, horsemanship, swordsmanship, and other athletic skills, before being promoted to knighthood at the age of 21.

COURT JESTER

Employed by the royal court to entertain the king, a jester would juggle, tell jokes, perform tricks, and generally clown around to improve his master's mood. In return, he was paid well, given a place to live, and enjoyed certain privileges, including being able to make fun of nobles and get away it!

BLACKSMITH

Every village had its own blacksmith, who would make everything from weapons and tools to door knobs and jewellery. Using charcoal as fuel, they would heat iron until it became malleable, then hammer it into various shapes on a heavy block known as an anvil.

RAT CATCHER

Rats were a big problem in Medieval Europe, spreading diseases and eating crops. Accompanied by a small dog or cat to sniff out the vermin, and various traps and poisons to capture or kill them, rat catchers would walk the streets and sewers, risking contracting the plague to earn a living.

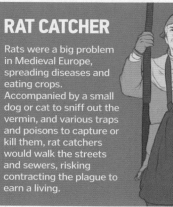

HERALD

With so many knights scattered across Europe, each with their own coat of arms, it was the job of a herald to keep track of them all. This also helped them in their other main duty: conducting and announcing the participants of jousting tournaments.

SCRIBE

As there were no printing presses in the Middle Ages, scribes would copy out text to create more copies of books. This was often done by monks, because they were literate, and it was hard work, as shown by the complaints they would write in the margins.

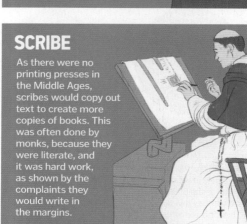

BARBER

Offering much more than a haircut, barbers would often perform medical procedures too. Known as barber surgeons, they would extract teeth, amputate limbs and carry out bloodletting, the practice of draining the blood to 'cure' various illnesses. With no anaesthetic or training, it was often a messy affair.

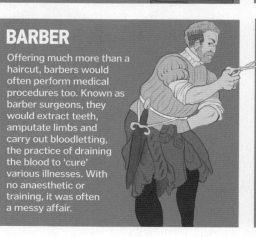

SPINSTER

In order for wool to be woven, it first had to be turned into yarn. This role was typically held by women, but male 'spinners' did also exist. They would first twist the fibres between their thumb and forefinger, then attach them to a drop-spindle, the weight of which would stretch the fibres into yarn as they spun.

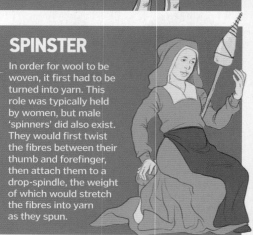

Illustrations • Rebekka Hearl

WHAT WAS FEUDALISM?

IN THE MEDIEVAL SYSTEM OF POWER, LAND WAS EXCHANGED FOR LOYALTY

In the Middle Ages, hard work got you nowhere. If you were born into a family of peasants, you would be expected to labour on farms but you would never own any land, and there was no social ladder to climb. That's because society in Medieval Europe was organised into different, closed groups according to status.

The king was at the very top, followed by barons, knights and peasants, and each group was bound by their roles and responsibilities. Today this is known as the feudal system, but the phrase was not used at the time, and there is much debate around whether Medieval society was so straightforward.

Nevertheless the feudal system serves as an analogy for the imbalanced structure of Medieval society. The king owned all the land and ruled as he wished, but over the centuries, the absolute monarchy has been overturned. In 13th-century England, for example, King John was forced to sign an agreement known as the Magna Carta, which limited his powers.

Feudalism was in decline all over Europe but it remained in France until the Revolution in 1789, and lasted until 1861 in Russia when serfdom (slavery) was finally abolished and all classes were given the right to own land for the first time.

A reproduction of a Medieval manuscript shows peasants sowing fields outside a walled town

DEATH OF FEUDALISM

The Black Death spread throughout Europe in the 14th century, killing an estimated 50 million people. It changed society for ever. One of these changes, it's been argued, was the breakdown of the feudal system. As the numbers of peasants dwindled, there were fewer people to work the land – the main source of wealth and power for the lords, and the foundation of the feudal system.

Those who survived the deadly disease seized their chance to get richer – from lands left by the dead and by demanding higher wages in return for labour. More money meant the lower classes could afford to dress like their social superiors and a law was passed in 1363 in a bid to stop this trend. The law put restrictions on the clothes and diets of people at every level of society, but it was impossible to enforce and it's been suggested that this led to the emergence of a middle class.

A woodcut of the plague showing Death looking triumphant

PYRAMIDS OF POWER

Medieval European and Japanese societies were built on similar, strict class systems

NOBILITY
Lords or barons reported to the king and were granted fiefs (portions of land), making them the second wealthiest class.

KING VS EMPEROR
The king had absolute power and rented lands to the barons in exchange for loyalty. In Japan, the emperor ruled but wielded little political power.

SHOGUN AND DAIMYOS
The Shogun was the real leader in Japan, with control over the military. He granted land to the Daimyo in exchange for loyalty as the Daimyo controlled the Samurai.

KNIGHTS VS SAMURAI
Japanese warriors known as Samurai served their Daimyo and protected their people, just as knights served the nobility who in turn provided them with food and lodging.

EUROPE

JAPAN

PEASANTS
The largest class in both Europe and Japanese societies worked the land. However in Japan they were ranked higher than merchants.

MERCHANTS
These were skilled workers who produced things like swords and clothes, but because peasants grew food, the merchants were seen as less important in Japanese society.

Illustrations • The Art Agency/Nick Sellers

HERALDRY

THE COLOURFUL GRAPHIC EMBLEMS THAT IDENTIFIED MEDIEVAL KNIGHTS AND ARE DISPLAYED BY THEIR DESCENDANTS TODAY

The image of a knight holding a shield bearing his coat of arms as he attempts to strike a blow to his opponent is a familiar one in the movies. In these Medieval tourneys, when the combatants wore full armour, these colourful emblems were the only way they could be identified. Much the same applied in warfare; the Bayeux Tapestry, which depicts the 1066 Battle of Hastings, appears to show a precursor of 'modern' heraldry on the battlefield.

Heraldry came about in an era when most people couldn't read or write. So instead of words, simple bold symbols were used to show the identity of the bearer. However, an essential requirement is that no two individuals share the same coat of arms. This requirement soon resulted in ever more complicated designs and, eventually, this led to the appointment of heraldic authorities to formalise the process. The job of the herald was to grant arms to individuals and to keep records, a task that continues today by Crown-appointed officers of arms in the College of Arms.

As part of the regulation of heraldry, a formal way of describing a coat of arms was devised. Called a blazon, this description is unique and unambiguous, providing sufficient information for a heraldic artist to reproduce the coat of arms. It can be something of a mystery to the uninitiated, though. The blazon for the coat or arms shown on the opposite page is "Quarterly: 1st and 4th, Argent three Lozenges conjoined in fess Gules within a Bordure Sable (Montagu); 2nd and 3rd, Or an Eagle displayed Vert beaked and membered Gules (Monthermer)". The strange turn of phrase results from the fact that not only is there a very precise way of describing things, but also because the vocabulary is a mixture of English, Norman French and Latin. Some of the words – for example Eagle and Bordure – are either English or French words that are easily recognisable, and some are heraldic words that really don't have everyday uses, such as lozenge, which is a diamond shape, or chevron, an inverted V.

The so-called 'tinctures' are puzzling, though. These are divided into colours: azure (blue), gules (red), sable (black), vert (green); metals – argent (silver) and or (gold); and furs – ermine, ermines, erminois, vair, vair ancient and counter-vair. It's also interesting that there are specific rules about how tinctures can be used. According to the rule of tincture, a coat of arms cannot have a colour on another colour or a metal on a metal so, for example, the coat of arms described as "Argent a chevron Or" (silver on a gold chevron) would not be allowed.

Heraldry might have its roots in the mists of time but if you want to get to grips with this ancient form of art, there's plenty of software to lend a hand. An interesting online resource can be found at drawshield.net. Here there's a tool for creating coats of arms and there's even a facility that attempts to draw one from a blazon.

> "SIMPLE BOLD SYMBOLS WERE USED TO SHOW THE IDENTITY OF THE BEARER"

THE COLLEGE OF ARMS

Re-established by royal charter in 1555 and occupying a building that dates back to the 1670s, the College of Arms is the official heraldic authority for England, Wales, Northern Ireland and much of the Commonwealth. As well as maintaining detailed registers of arms, pedigrees and genealogies, the College is also responsible for the granting of new coats of arms to qualified bearers.

The College of Arms is comprised of 13 officers of arms, the most senior of which are the Kings of Arms. Under the authority of the Crown, the Kings of Arms have the power to grant new coats of arms to both individuals and corporate bodies.

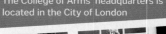

The College of Arms' headquarters is located in the City of London

In Medieval tournaments, heraldry allowed the combatants to be identified even though they were encased in armour

THE RIGHT TO BEAR ARMS

It's commonly thought that people are entitled to bear a coat of arms that's associated with their family name. Lots of companies offer products featuring your 'family coat of arms', but this is just playing in to the common misconception that arms are connected to surnames. People with the same name might be entitled to completely different arms, while others of that name will be entitled to no coat of arms at all. Instead, coats of arms were granted to individuals – as they still are today – and are passed on through the male line of descent. It's possible that you might be entitled to bear arms, but to be sure you'd need to carry out some detective work in tracing your ancestry.

There's no such thing as a family coat of arms

Image Source • P. Sonard

Containing 719 separate coats of arms, the Stowe armorial is an extreme example of quartering

THE HERALDIC ACHIEVEMENT

The heraldic components to which a bearer of arms is entitled to display

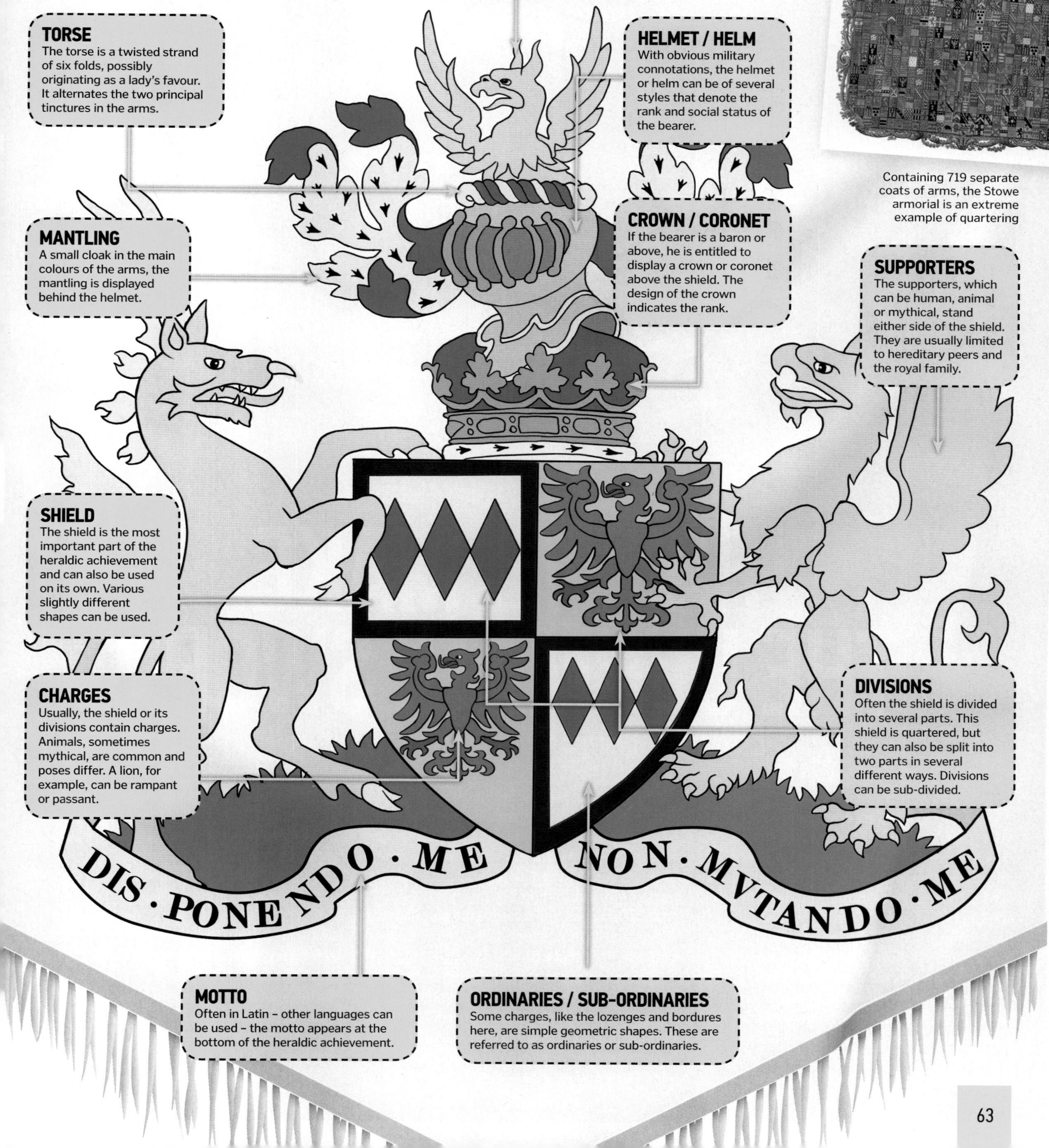

CREST
Originally a decorative sculpture worn by knights in tournaments, the crest is the top-most part of the heraldic achievement and often takes the form of an animal.

TORSE
The torse is a twisted strand of six folds, possibly originating as a lady's favour. It alternates the two principal tinctures in the arms.

HELMET / HELM
With obvious military connotations, the helmet or helm can be of several styles that denote the rank and social status of the bearer.

MANTLING
A small cloak in the main colours of the arms, the mantling is displayed behind the helmet.

CROWN / CORONET
If the bearer is a baron or above, he is entitled to display a crown or coronet above the shield. The design of the crown indicates the rank.

SUPPORTERS
The supporters, which can be human, animal or mythical, stand either side of the shield. They are usually limited to hereditary peers and the royal family.

SHIELD
The shield is the most important part of the heraldic achievement and can also be used on its own. Various slightly different shapes can be used.

CHARGES
Usually, the shield or its divisions contain charges. Animals, sometimes mythical, are common and poses differ. A lion, for example, can be rampant or passant.

DIVISIONS
Often the shield is divided into several parts. This shield is quartered, but they can also be split into two parts in several different ways. Divisions can be sub-divided.

DIS · PONENDO · ME   NON · MVTANDO · ME

MOTTO
Often in Latin – other languages can be used – the motto appears at the bottom of the heraldic achievement.

ORDINARIES / SUB-ORDINARIES
Some charges, like the lozenges and bordures here, are simple geometric shapes. These are referred to as ordinaries or sub-ordinaries.

Illustration • Rebekka Hearl

63

Image Source • Joe Cummings

HOW TO MAKE THE ULTIMATE SWORD

DISCOVER THE ANCIENT ART OF FORGING A DEADLY WEAPON

Swords were the first tools designed solely to kill. There were other weapons before them, such as spears, axes and knives, but they were all originally intended for other purposes before being adopted as instruments of war. The spear was initially made for hunting and the axe for chopping wood, while knives have many functions. But the sword exists only to kill people.

Initially, swords were as much status items as weapons. These first swords, appearing from around 3000 BCE, were forged from bronze, an alloy of copper and tin. As the technology required to forge bronze was still new, and

bronze itself quite rare, these early swords were very uncommon, highly prized and a sign that the person carrying them was extraordinarily wealthy and powerful. One such example is the bronze sword, shaped like a sickle, that was buried with Tutankhamun circa 1327 BCE. Called a khopesh, the sword of the pharaoh was sharpened on its outside edge, with the tip used both as a hook and a club.

The technology to make bronze spread around the Mediterranean basin, and trade evolved to bring tin from mines in the Iberian Peninsula and Cornwall to the forges of the eastern Mediterranean. As a result, swords

became more and more widespread, until whole armies carried them. The Minoan, Sumerian and Assyrian empires were all carved out by armies carrying bronze swords.

But iron changed everything. The metal itself is common, strong and durable, and will produce a weapon that is both flexible and tough. The Hittites were early adopters of this technology, using iron weapons to form their empire from 1600 BCE onwards. With the Hittites showing the way, iron became the new material from which to forge swords.

The problem with iron swords, though, is that iron bends. To make a sharp, hard, cutting edge, you need steel – an alloy of iron and carbon. In the first millennium BCE, the Etruscans began to create alloys of steel and iron, making swords that had edges hard enough to cut through armour, yet which were also sufficiently flexible to withstand the shock of battle.

The Romans developed Etruscan technology, creating the blade that characterised the Roman military machine: the gladius. This short, stabbing sword was the weapon of the legionary and, armed with it, the Romans created their empire. But it was the longer sword employed by their cavalry, the spatha, that outlived Roman rule. As the Western Empire declined, many of the barbarian groups who were employed to defend it used the spatha. The weapon became the prototype from which the swords of the Anglo-Saxons and Vikings, the high points of Western sword making, developed.

Perhaps the finest example of these swords is the one found at Bamburgh in Northumberland. Excavated in 1960 and rediscovered in 2001 (just in time, as it was about to be thrown into a skip), the Bamburgh Sword was forged in the 7th century. About 76 centimetres (two feet six inches) long when first made, it was passed

down through the centuries until, some 300 years after it was forged, it broke. As an heirloom of kings and earls, the sword was not thrown away, but buried, until archaeologists excavated it, although at first they did not realise what they had found.

The Bamburgh Sword was made from six strands of iron, pattern-welded together. No other sword has been found with more than four. In pattern welding, the iron strands are heated, twisted and hammered together, over and over again. When finished, pattern-welded swords have striking swirling designs on them.

It was this tell-tale pattern that led, in part, to the end of pattern-welded swords. Every warrior wanted a weapon like this and, by the later Viking Age, armies had grown to 1,000 or more men. In response, crafty swordsmiths began producing fake versions of these blades, which had an ordinary iron core and a thin pattern-welded layer on top.

With the arrival of massed armies, swordsmiths started to forge simpler, easier-to-make blades. The design of the swords continued to change through the following centuries, to suit the fighting styles of the men

carrying them. Blade styles also changed as armour improved, making it harder to cut through with a sword's edge. As a result, the point of the sword became more important, being sharpened and hardened so that it could punch a hole through an enemy's armour. Despite bullets largely replacing blades on battlefields, swords continued to be employed by soldiers into the 20th century, being used widely during the Russian Civil War (1918-20) and the Sino-Japanese War (1937-45).

A historical reenactor dressed as an Anglo-Saxon warrior, armed with sword and seax

BLADES THROUGH THE AGES

Gladius
The sword that conquered the world. This was the sword of the Roman legions, designed for thrusting, and used when standing in phalanx (rectangular) formation beside other legionaries.

Image Source • Albion Europe ApS

Spatha
The sword that was used by Roman cavalry. It was longer than the gladiu,s and in the later Roman Empire it gradually started to replace the gladius as the main infantry weapon.

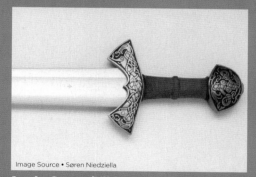
Image Source • Søren Niedziella

Anglo-Saxon/Viking swords
These swords evolved from the spatha and were used for hand-to-hand combat. Anglo-Saxon and Viking smiths perfected the design, making some of the finest swords in history.

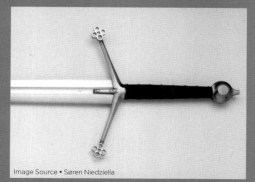
Image Source • Søren Niedziella

Claymore
This was an two-handed sword used in Scotland from around 1400 to 1700. It was approximately 140 centimetres (four feet seven inches) long, making it a terrifying presence on any battlefield.

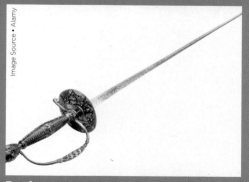

Rapier
The rapier was a sword carried by civilians in the 16th and 17th centuries, designed for self-defence, and used in brawls and duels. Modern fencing has developed from the style of fighting used it.

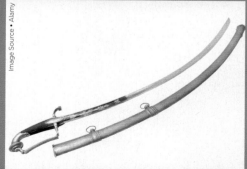

Sabre
The sabre is usually a curved, single-edged sword used by cavalry in the Napoleonic Wars. However, they could also be straight blades, used in thrusting attacks. Both were devastating against infantry.

FORGING THE BLADE
HOW TO MAKE THE PERFECT KILLING MACHINE

Swordsmiths throughout history have faced a big problem when making their weapons. Iron is flexible, and this makes it excellent as a blade, since it will bend when struck, rather than breaking in combat – half a sword is not much use in a battle! But because iron is malleable, it will not keep an edge, meaning that after half an hour's fighting, a pure iron sword will turn into something little better than a long club.

Steel (an alloy of iron and carbon) is much harder, so it will keep its edge even after slicing through shields and armour. But steel is also brittle, making it vulnerable to sideways, parrying blows. A sharp steel sword will cut through almost anything, but a good whack with a wooden staff would probably break it.

Through the centuries, swordsmiths have attempted to marry the strengths of steel and iron, and to minimise their weaknesses by forging swords with iron cores and steel cutting edges. Welding core and edge together was – and is – a hugely skilled process, and it can go wrong at any stage if impurities concentrate at a point. This can be particularly upsetting for a swordsmith who has spent days hammer-forging a blade, so a lot of patience and technique are needed.

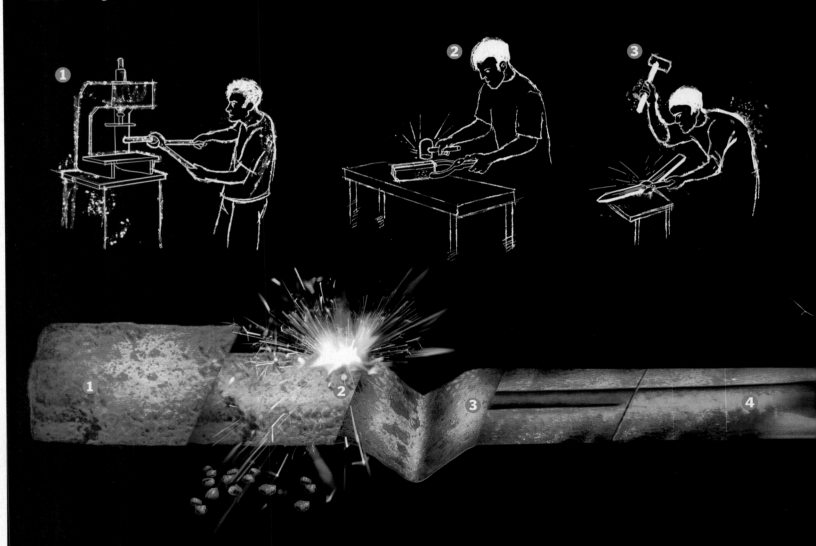

STEP 1
CHOOSE YOUR METAL
The iron made the sword. Getting the best metal was the most important part of making a good blade. However, apart from the occasional meteorite, there is very little pure iron on Earth. For swordmaking, iron was often obtained from bogs or mined; bog iron is carried in liquid form into the bog, then concentrated by anaerobic bacteria, producing small lumps of the metal. This source is renewable, as new lumps appear in 15 to 20 years.

STEP 2
FORGING
Forging is when the smith hits the hot metal with a hammer over and over again, working it into shape. The best swords fuse iron and steel, and heating the metals makes thousands of tiny welds, joining the two materials together. Forging also spreads any impurities evenly through the sword, reducing the chance of the weapon breaking. In the best swords, bars of good iron are twisted together, further spreading out any impurities. The bars are welded into a solid core, and the steel edge welded on to the core.

STEP 3
ANNEALING

As the swordsmith is forging the blade, they will usually return it to the heat several times, and let it cool again without working on it. This helps to reduce irregularities in the blade. Once it has been shaped, the sword is annealed by heating it to a precise temperature and allowing it to cool very slowly. This is done either by allowing the forge fire to cool, or by burying the sword in hot sand.

STEP 4
GRINDING

Swordsmiths through the centuries have used different methods to grind the blade, from water-powered wheels to sand on leather, but hand files were the most common tools employed. The aim of grinding is to remove the material that cannot easily be removed by the forging process. The fuller – the groove down the middle of the sword – and any engraved designs are also added at this stage.

STEP 5
HARDENING

The shaped sword is reheated until it glows a dull orange colour. At this heat, the metal becomes non-magnetic. The sword is then quenched in water. This helps to line up the crystalline structure of the iron and steel in the sword and makes it harder. But quenching can also make the sword brittle. To overcome this, smiths must heat the blade again, for the next stage in making the sword.

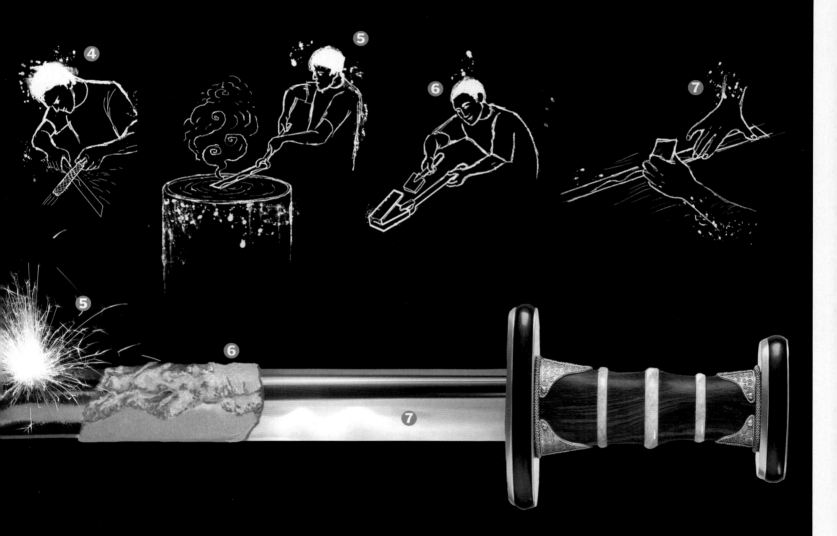

STEP 6
TEMPERING

To overcome the brittleness produced in the hardening, the sword has to be reheated to a lower temperature than before. In the days before temperature gauges, this was done by colour; the smith heats the sword until the edge is a straw colour, and the centre – with its thicker metal – a deep purple. The blade is then slowly cooled to reintroduce some flexibility, making sure it does not break in battle.

STEP 7
COMPLETION

Although the sword is now forged, it looks dirty and crusted, so it has to be cleaned. Abrasives, such as sand on leather, are used to file and clean it, until it is ready for sharpening on a whetstone. After a final sharpen, pattern-welded swords are etched to highlight the pattern on the blade. The most impressive swords have hilts made of precious metals, with jewels inset, while the pommel and guard are adjusted to keep the weapon balanced. The sword is now ready for use.

THE PORCELAIN TOWER OF NANJING

THE CONSTRUCTION, DESTRUCTION AND REVIVAL OF A MEDIEVAL WONDER

In early 15th-century China, the Yongle Emperor of the Ming dynasty ordered the construction of a towering monument to honour his mother. The Porcelain Tower was a grand pagoda built in the city of Nanjing – the imperial capital at the time – as part of the grand Bao'en Buddhist Temple complex.

The tower was constructed from white porcelain bricks, which would have glistened in the sunlight, and it wasadorned with vibrant glazed designs of animals, flowers and landscapes in greens, yellows and browns. Historians studying the remnants suggest that the glazed porcelain bricks were made by highly skilled workers, but sadly the methods used to make them have been lost to history.

Some of the largest bricks were more than 50 centimetres (one foot seven inches) thick and weighed as much as 150 kilograms (330 pounds) each, with the coloured glazes staying bright for centuries. Nowadays, workers trying to replicate them struggle to make anything larger than five centimetres (two inches) thick and their colours fade after just a decade.

The tower was widely regarded as the most beautiful pagoda in China, and it became renowned as one of the seven wonders of the Medieval world, featuring in the records of Westerners who travelled to the region. It was also one of the tallest buildings in the area until it was almost completely reduced to rubble during the Taiping Rebellion in 1856.

REBUILDING THE WONDER

Today, the old and new stand side by side at the Porcelain Tower Heritage Park. The reconstructed tower (made from steel girders and glass rather than porcelain) overlooks the museum housing the original blocks of the Nanjing Tower door.

The new high-tech replica provides an interactive experience, as visitors are encouraged to use a smartphone to scan QR codes for more information about the site. The incredible interior of the new building immortalises the historical and cultural significance of the original medieval tower in mesmerising displays of sound and light, including a room of thousands of light bulbs that change colour. The new tower also offers 360-degree views of the city as it overlooks a landscape of rivers and architecture.

Image Source • Whisper of the heart

Businessman Wang Jianlin reportedly funded the replica's construction with a donation of 1bn yuan

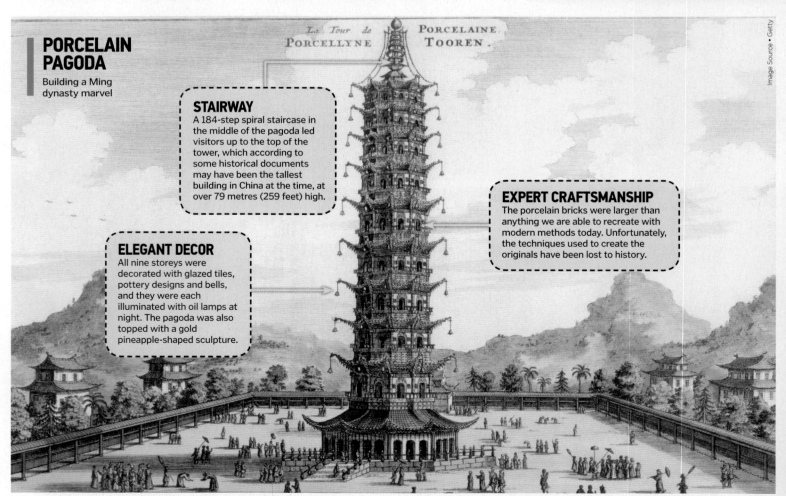

Image Source • Getty

La Tour de Porcelaine
PORCELLYNE TOOREN.

PORCELAIN PAGODA

Building a Ming dynasty marvel

STAIRWAY
A 184-step spiral staircase in the middle of the pagoda led visitors up to the top of the tower, which according to some historical documents may have been the tallest building in China at the time, at over 79 metres (259 feet) high.

EXPERT CRAFTSMANSHIP
The porcelain bricks were larger than anything we are able to recreate with modern methods today. Unfortunately, the techniques used to create the originals have been lost to history.

ELEGANT DECOR
All nine storeys were decorated with glazed tiles, pottery designs and bells, and they were each illuminated with oil lamps at night. The pagoda was also topped with a gold pineapple-shaped sculpture.

ALCHEMY

THE ANCIENT PRACTICE OF TRYING TO TURN LEAD INTO GOLD WAS THE PROTOSCIENCE THAT GAVE BIRTH TO MODERN CHEMISTRY

The origin of alchemy lies in ancient Egypt, where the cultures of the ancient Greeks and Arabs melded together and the first alchemists began by making glass, medicines and metals. They wanted to understand the secrets of the world around them and were searching for the prima materia, the matter from which all other matter was created. Sulphur, mercury and salt were considered to be the three heavenly substances.

In the 14th century, a Spanish alchemist who took the name Geber after the 8th-century Arab alchemist Jabir ibn Hayyan helped to spread alchemy across Renaissance Europe. He believed that all metals were made from mercury and sulphur, and that copper, lead, iron, silver and tin could all be transformed into gold with the help of the philosopher's stone – a concept known as chrysopoeia.

This, along with the elixir of life, was the major focus of alchemy, but behind the myth and magic was some real science. Geber learned to make stronger acids by distilling vinegar to drive off the excess water; Swiss-German alchemist Paracelsus (born Theophrastus von Hohenheim) invented an opium painkiller called laudanum; and in 1669, German alchemist Hennig Brand (depicted below) boiled urine and discovered a white material that glowed green in the dark: phosphorous.

But alchemy wasn't just confined to Europe. Alchemists in China and India had also been experimenting, inventing black powder, forging steel and discovering that flames changed colour depending on which metal was burnt. But in 1661, it all started to change.

Irish alchemist Robert Boyle published a book titled *The Sceptical Chymist* that called for a more scientific approach to their work, and after decades of study chemistry finally started to appear in its modern form. In the 19th century, French chemist Antoine Lavoisier laid down the theory of the conservation of mass, explaining that matter cannot be created or destroyed and debunking alchemical myths once and for all.

PHYSICIST OR ALCHEMIST?

Sir Isaac Newton is best known as the genius physicist and mathematician behind the law of universal gravitation, the laws of motion, calculus and the reflecting telescope, but this great scientist was also an alchemist. In fact, he wrote more about alchemy than he did about any other subject. But in the 1700s alchemy was taboo and his work on the subject was buried after he died.

In 2016, a closer look at his writings revealed hints that he was working on the fabled philosopher's stone. Alchemists thought that this object would turn cheap metals into gold and might also hold the secret to eternal life. Within Newton's manuscripts is a recipe for one of the key ingredients, philosophic mercury, and historians think that it's likely he tried to make it as part of his experiments.

There are hundreds more pages of Newton's writings just waiting to be explored

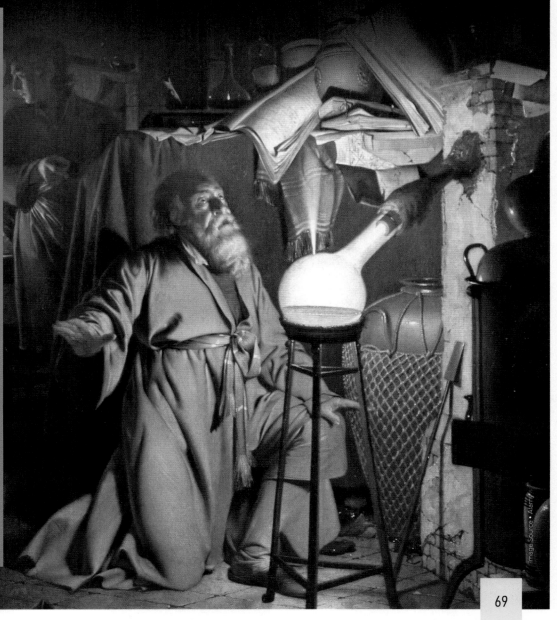

Image Source • Alamy

CIRCUMNAVIGATING THE GLOBE

THE INTREPID EXPLORERS WHOSE EXPEDITIONS LED THEM AROUND THE WORLD

Words by **Charlie Evans**

On 6 September 1522, the tattered ship Victoria sailed into the port of Sanlúcar de Barrameda. Its sails were badly torn, and it was only being kept afloat by the continuous pumping out of the water that was filling up its hull. The crew had been months without food. As they sailed back home to Spain they had been forced to resort to killing and eating rats that were infesting the ship and drinking putrid water that had been stored for months. Over the previous three years they had survived mutiny, execution, disease, starvation and dehydration.

Victoria was one of five ships that had set out to find a new route to the Spice Islands, but it was the only ship to return, carrying its starving crew of just 18 men. These men were the first to navigate around the entire world – a feat that would not be accomplished for another 58 years.

The earliest circumnavigations were driven by curiosity, fame and wealth; sailors would discover new lands and trade routes, and they would return home as heroes. But humans were not content with just mastering circumnavigation on water. Instead, our

expeditions and our ambitions were to become even bigger. First we conquered circumnavigation by sea, and then we took to the skies, before Soviet cosmonaut Yuri Gagarin faced the final frontier and completed the first orbit of the Earth in space.

A global circumnavigation is generally recognised as a great circular route that passes through at least one pair of points on the opposite sides of the Earth to each other. The rules for a round-the-world sailing record dictate that the length of the voyage must be at least 21,600 nautical miles and that the

Image Source • Getty

equator must be crossed at some point along the journey. Today we have more technology to keep circumnavigators safe, their supplies stocked up and their journey more comfortable. This includes accurate GPS systems and extensive maps to guide them, advanced weather warnings, knowledge about political situations, extensive maps and robust ships.

The first ships built for circumnavigation were carracks: three- or four-masted ocean-going sailing ships that were large enough to stay stable in rough seas and carry enough cargo and provisions for long voyages. Sailors would rely on equipment and (inaccurate) maps to navigate their route. In addition to their basic magnetic compass they used a backstaff to measure the angle of the shadow of the Moon or Sun to determine latitude measurements and assist them with navigating the oceans. They also relied on a lead line that was dropped into the water to touch the ocean floor, which was marked and pulled back up to measure how deep the ocean was at that point.

Modern circumnavigators have replaced most of this kit with high-tech versions that calculate the same information, such as a gyro compass, which is more accurate and is not affected by an external magnetic field. Modern ships are also fitted with Automatic Radar Plotting Aids that display the position of a ship and any vessels nearby to prevent collisions. Echo sounders are also used instead of lead line. They work by bouncing sound waves off the ocean floor to measure the depth of the water below the ship.

If you're feeling inspired, you don't actually need to learn how to sail a boat or start building up your leg muscles to hit the road with a bike. Instead, you could circumnavigate the world using only commercial flights. It just takes quite a bit of money and some careful planning, particularly to limit the amount of time you're hanging around in airports, but you could even attempt to set a new record.

The record for doing this is held by David Springbett, who completed a 37,124-kilometre (23,067-mile) circumnavigation (under FAI regulations) in just 44 hours and six minutes back in 1980. Unfortunately, you're probably not going to be able to beat his record today because he had a massive advantage; some of his journey was made in one of the fastest passenger planes in history, Concorde, which could reach speeds of 2,160 kilometres (1,342 miles) per hour. The fastest routes using modern aircraft would take over 50 hours.

However you choose to circumnavigate the world, you probably won't have the same fate as Magellan and his crew thanks to the new technology we have at our fingertips.

HISTORIC FIRSTS IN CIRCUMNAVIGATION

Whether on land, over sea or in space, these pioneering journeys were driven by curiosity, determination and a hunger for adventure

1,083 DAYS

SHIP 1519–1522 MAGELLAN'S CREW

21 DAYS, 5 HOURS AND 31 MINUTES

ZEPPELIN 1929 DR HUGO ECKENER

19 DAYS, 21 HOURS AND 55 MINUTES

HOT AIR BALLOON 1999 BERTRAND PICCARD AND BRIAN JONES

175 DAYS

PLANE (WITH STOPS) 1924 LTS. LOWELL SMITH, LESLIE ARNOLD, LTS. ERIK NELSON AND JOHN HARDING JR.

94 HOURS AND 1 MINUTE

PLANE (NON-STOP) 1949 CAPTAIN JAMES GALLAGHER

9 DAYS, 3 MINUTES AND 44 SECONDS

PLANE (NON-STOP, NO REFUELLING) 1986 DICK RUTAN AND JEANA YEAGER

108 MINUTES

SPACECRAFT 1961 YURI GAGARIN

In 1987, the Indian Army Corps of Engineers completed the first circumnavigation by an Indian crew on a yacht called Trishna

> "THEY HAD LEARNT THAT THE WORLD WAS A GLOBE, NOT FLAT AS WAS BELIEVED AT THE TIME, AND THEY DISCOVERED NEW ISLANDS THAT HAD NEVER BEEN MAPPED"

Image Source • Ayepee99

MAGELLAN'S CIRCUMNAVIGATION OF THE WORLD

Ferdinand Magellan had one goal when he sailed from Seville on 10 August 1519: he wanted to find a western trade route for Spain to the Spice (Maluku) Islands. This small cluster of islands to the northeast of Indonesia had become an important location to source nutmeg and cloves – spices that were worth 1,000 per cent more than their cost in the Spice Islands.

270 men joined Magellan's voyage in five ships: Trinidad, San Antonio, Conception, Santiago and Victoria. Trinidad was the flagship and commanded by Magellan himself. They sailed from Spain to South America, across the South Pacific Ocean to Oceania, before reaching Southeast Asia, crossing the Indian Ocean to Africa, eventually sailing along Africa's west coast back up to Spain.

They had lost most of their crew, but they had made great discoveries. They had learnt that the world was a globe, not flat as was believed at the time, and they discovered new islands that had never been mapped. Most importantly,

they had established a new trade route for the Spanish to reach the Spice Islands and had returned with one ship filled with a king's ransom in cinnamon and cloves.

This illustration of the Trinidad was drawn by Abraham Ortelius

Image Source • Abraham Ortelius

Prima ego velivolis ambivi cursibus Orbem,
Magellane novo te duce ducta freto.

MARGARITA ISLAND
The largest island in the Venezuelan state of Nueva Esparta in the Caribbean Sea has recently seen a spate of pirate boardings in the area, and most ships avoid the route.

THE INTERTROPICAL CONVERGENCE ZONE
This area is where winds from the Northern and Southern hemispheres meet, which can cause violent and unpredictable thunderstorms that could pose a threat to aircraft.

CAPE HORN
The storms off Cape Horn make the area difficult and often impossible to navigate. Sailors who do attempt to use the route risk having their ship grounded on the rocks off the coast.

DRAKE PASSAGE
Drake Passage at the southern tip of South America is one of the roughest seas in the world and has been responsible for many shipwrecks.

THE CHALLENGES OF CIRCUMNAVIGATION
STORMS, PIRATES, AND ROUGH SEAS –
TRAVELLING THE GLOBE IS NO EASY FEAT

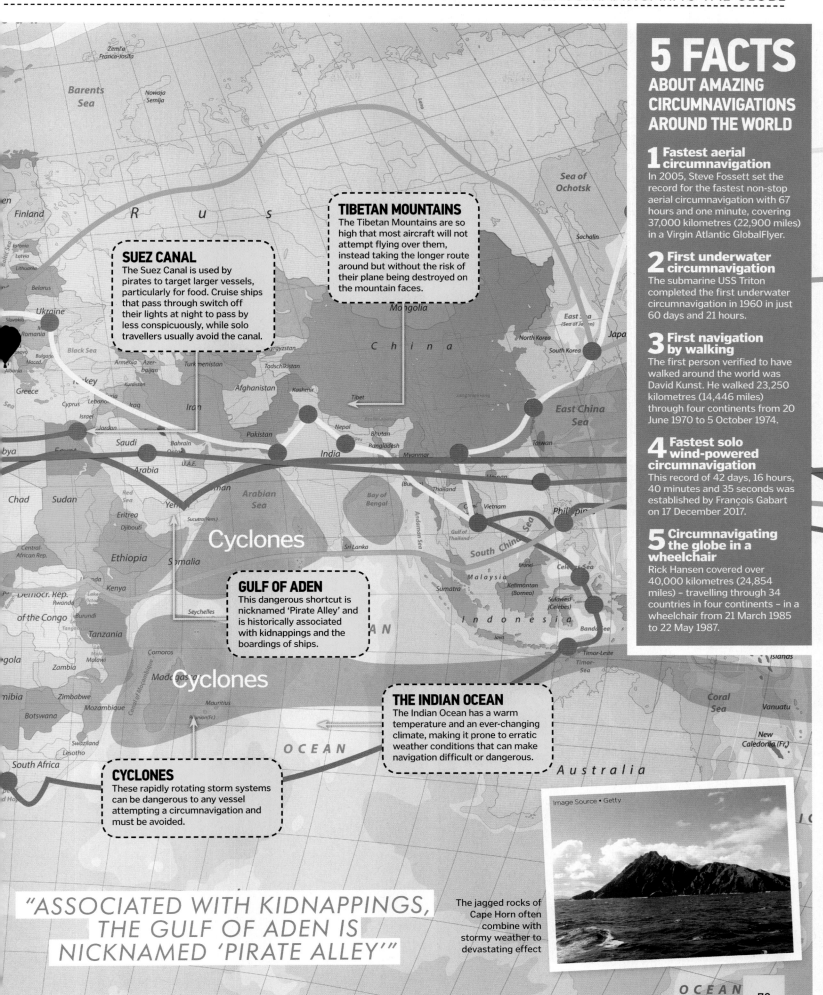

5 FACTS
ABOUT AMAZING CIRCUMNAVIGATIONS AROUND THE WORLD

1 Fastest aerial circumnavigation

In 2005, Steve Fossett set the record for the fastest non-stop aerial circumnavigation with 67 hours and one minute, covering 37,000 kilometres (22,900 miles) in a Virgin Atlantic GlobalFlyer.

2 First underwater circumnavigation

The submarine USS Triton completed the first underwater circumnavigation in 1960 in just 60 days and 21 hours.

3 First navigation by walking

The first person verified to have walked around the world was David Kunst. He walked 23,250 kilometres (14,446 miles) through four continents from 20 June 1970 to 5 October 1974.

4 Fastest solo wind-powered circumnavigation

This record of 42 days, 16 hours, 40 minutes and 35 seconds was established by François Gabart on 17 December 2017.

5 Circumnavigating the globe in a wheelchair

Rick Hansen covered over 40,000 kilometres (24,854 miles) – travelling through 34 countries in four continents – in a wheelchair from 21 March 1985 to 22 May 1987.

TIBETAN MOUNTAINS
The Tibetan Mountains are so high that most aircraft will not attempt flying over them, instead taking the longer route around but without the risk of their plane being destroyed on the mountain faces.

SUEZ CANAL
The Suez Canal is used by pirates to target larger vessels, particularly for food. Cruise ships that pass through switch off their lights at night to pass by less conspicuously, while solo travellers usually avoid the canal.

GULF OF ADEN
This dangerous shortcut is nicknamed 'Pirate Alley' and is historically associated with kidnappings and the boardings of ships.

THE INDIAN OCEAN
The Indian Ocean has a warm temperature and an ever-changing climate, making it prone to erratic weather conditions that can make navigation difficult or dangerous.

CYCLONES
These rapidly rotating storm systems can be dangerous to any vessel attempting a circumnavigation and must be avoided.

Cyclones

Cyclones

Image Source • Getty

The jagged rocks of Cape Horn often combine with stormy weather to devastating effect

"ASSOCIATED WITH KIDNAPPINGS, THE GULF OF ADEN IS NICKNAMED 'PIRATE ALLEY'"

MODERN HISTORY

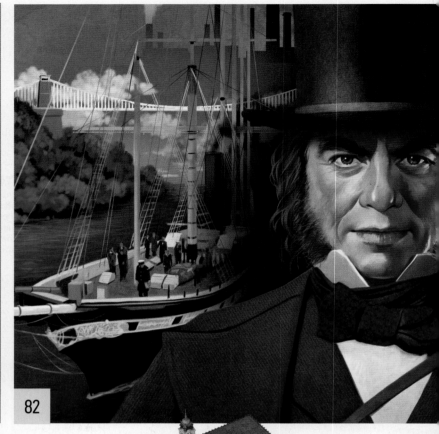

82

76

94

76

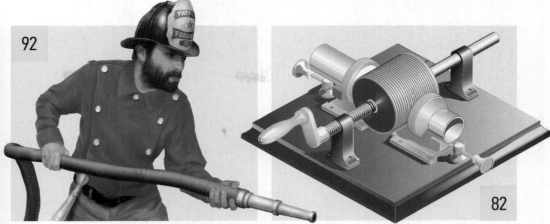

92

82

93

86

94

HOW THE BATTLE OF WATERLOO WAS WON

WHEN NAPOLEON BONAPARTE RETURNED FROM EXILE TO RECLAIM HIS EMPIRE, STANDING IN HIS WAY WERE TWO DETERMINED COALITION ARMIES

Image Source • Joe Cummings

In 1814, Napoleon Bonaparte, emperor of France and conqueror of Europe, was finally defeated and exiled to Elba in the Mediterranean Sea. However, just over ten months later, he escaped his island prison and landed on the south coast of France on 1 March 1815 to reclaim his lost empire. He gathered supporters, and armies sent by King Louis XVIII to challenge him quickly changed sides, declaring their loyalty to the returned emperor.

The news of Napoleon's return shocked the continent and before long, a new coalition of European nations was lined up against him. Both the duke of Wellington, commanding an Anglo-Allied force, and Gebhard Leberecht von Blücher, leading a Prussian army, moved to intercept the French, who were mounting an invasion of Belgium.

Wellington knew he could not defeat Napoleon's army alone. The French slightly outnumbered his Anglo-Allied force, which was made up of British, Dutch, German and Belgian troops, plus a number of men from other nations. Further to the east, Blücher commanded roughly 115,000 men, which would be enough to tip the balance against Napoleon – if only the two armies could reach each other in time. Realising this, Napoleon was determined to drive a wedge between his enemies, using his superior numbers to defeat each in turn.

On 16 June, this strategy almost worked. At around 2pm, French Field Marshal Michel Ney attacked Wellington at Quatre Bras, the location of a vital crossroads along the road to Brussels. Further east at Ligny, Blücher was attacked by Napoleon and forced to retreat north. Napoleon ordered one of his generals, Marshal Emmanuel de Grouchy, to pursue the Prussian force closely, while he returned to Ney at Quatre Bras, who had allowed Wellington to escape.

Withdrawing north, the duke halted on the night of 17 June and headquartered in the village of Waterloo. Not far behind, Napoleon and his army made camp further south, and the emperor rested at a farm called La Caillou. Heavy rainfall all through the night soaked both armies and turned much of the ground between them into a muddy quagmire. This would prove critical the following morning.

Waking with full confidence, Napoleon declared to his generals that defeating Wellington would be "as easy as having breakfast". Wellington, meanwhile, had been surveying his battle lines with his staff, identifying the key positions (three farmhouses) that his troops would have to hold. He deployed a majority of his men and cannons behind the raised ridgeline of Mont-Saint-Jean, which was an advantageous position to defend.

At 11am he ordered Marshal Honoré Charles Reille's II Corps to occupy the woods close to the farmhouse of Hougoumont. Men of the Coldstream Guards and Nassau regiments were garrisoned in this building and its adjoining orchard and garden. The defenders had created holes in the walls of the courtyard through which they could fire on the enemy.

Although Napoleon only intended this attack as a diversion to distract Wellington from the main French offensive, it soon became a costly bloodbath as the attack turned into an all-out assault to take Hougoumont. At one critical point a number of French soldiers broke into the building's courtyard through the north gate.

Lieutenant Colonel James Macdonell, the garrison commander, rallied his men and managed to shut the gate on the enemy.

The struggle for Hougoumont would last for the rest of the day. Perhaps due to fierce artillery bombardment, parts of the compound were set on fire. Seeing this, Wellington ordered his men to occupy and defend the ruins – he knew Hougoumont had to be held at all costs.

While Wellington's right flank endured wave after wave of attacks, the centre-left of his battle line was soon under pressure. At around 2pm the French I Corps, commanded by the Comte d'Erlon, began its advance against the farms of La Haye Sainte and Papelotte, advancing up the

BATTLE OF WATERLOO STATS

FRENCH ARMY NUMBERED
72,000
FRENCH LOSSES (KILLED OR WOUNDED)
25,000
CAPTURED
8,000–9,000

ALLIED ARMY (UNDER WELLINGTON)
68,000
ALLIED LOSSES
KILLED
3,500
MISSING
3,300
WOUNDED
10,000+

PRUSSIAN ARMY NUMBERED
50,000
PRUSSIAN LOSSES (KILLED OR WOUNDED)
7,000

2–3 MILES
LENGTH OF ALLIED FRONT

60,000
HORSES FEATURED IN THE BATTLE

APPROX.
400
CANNONS USED
(250 FRENCH, 150 ALLIED)

ONE THIRD
WELLINGTON'S ARMY WAS BRITISH. THE REST WAS PREDOMINANTLY GERMAN, INTERSPERSED WITH SOME DUTCH UNITS

'Scotland Forever' – an 1881 painting by Lady Butler depicting the charge of the Scots Greys during the battle

EMPEROR NAPOLEON BONAPARTE

Born on the Mediterranean island of Corsica in 1769, Napoleon travelled to France during the revolution, serving as an artillery officer. His tactical awareness and leadership were soon apparent, and by 1796 he was in command of an army and leading a campaign in Italy. In 1799, after returning from campaigning in Egypt, Napoleon seized control of the disorganised government in Paris and later in 1804 crowned himself emperor of the French. As emperor, he established the Bank of France and passed widespread law reform, much of which has survived centuries. He also gave powerful positions to many of his close family, including crowning his brother Jérôme king of Italy. He married his second wife, Marie-Louise, in 1810, and his son, Napoleon II, was born in 1811. After his final defeat at the Battle of Waterloo, the emperor abdicated and was later exiled to the South Atlantic island of Saint Helena, where he died in 1821.

Napoleon, painted in military uniform, in his study at the Tuileries Palace

ridgeline towards the waiting defenders. Approximately 17,000–20,000 French infantrymen advanced in huge columns, beating drums and cheering "Vive l'empereur!" ("Long live the emperor!"). Once they reached the brow of the ridge, they were met with horrific volley fire from batallions of British and German soldiers.

The duke had stretched his infantry holding the ridge – approximately 3,500 men – into three ranks of up to 150 soldiers wide. This gave the defenders as much firepower as possible to halt the French advance. Most soldiers were armed with a 'Brown Bess' flintlock musket, which had an effective range of just 40-50 metres (131-164 feet). As these firearms were very inaccurate, a massed volley of shots was the most effective way of inflicting casualties.

Once the distance between the two forces had closed, the 5th Division commander General Thomas Picton ordered his men to fix bayonets and charge the French, crying, "Charge! Charge! Hurrah! Hurrah!" The general

was killed instantly, but his counterattack drove the French back.

Watching these events unfold was Lord Uxbridge, commander of the British cavalry. Seeing an opportunity, he ordered a massive cavalry charge, which successfully destroyed d'Erlon's advance. Hundreds of men were cut down or sent fleeing by the cavalry, which gained momentum as the horses galloped down the slope, where the French infantry had only recently marched.

Although a decisive moment, this charge came at a huge cost. Many cavalrymen continued to gallop across the field towards the French cannons, where fresh French cavalry quickly counter-attacked and inflicted heavy casualties on the tired British.

With the British cavalry all but eliminated, the French cuirassiers, or heavy cavalry, were ordered to attack the Anglo-Allied infantry over the ridge. Ordinarily, cavalry held a huge advantage over foot soldiers, especially when attacking thin lines of men, who would often

HOW THE BATTLE UNFOLDED

Blow-by-blow, from the first shots until the final victory

01:00–03:00
NIGHT DEPLOYMENT
The two armies make camp – Napoleon sets up his headquarters at La Caillou farm in the south and Wellington finds quarters in the village of Waterloo to the north.

09:00
DELAYED ATTACK
With heavy rain overnight, Napoleon decides to wait for the battleground to dry out before beginning his attack.

11:20–11:30
GRANDE BATTERIE OPENS FIRE
The French cannons begin firing on the Anglo-Allied positions, who promptly return fire. French infantry begin advancing on Hougoumont.

12:00–13:20
ALL-OUT ASSAULT
French infantry continue to attack Hougoumont on Wellington's right flank, while around 17–20,000 men of d'Erlon's Corps march against the left flank.

panic, break ranks and be easily chased down. However, what Napoleon and his generals could not see over the ridgeline of Mont-Saint-Jean was that Wellington had arranged his infantry battalions into 24-by-30 square formations. Each square presented bayonets and muskets pointed outward at every side, posing an impossible obstacle for cavalry to break. Nonetheless, the French horses swept over the ridge and poured in among the formations, seeking any gap in the lines. For two hours the French charged back and forth over the ridge to try and destroy the British formations, which held, the horsemen caught in deadly crossfire.

From around 4.30pm, Napoleon had even more troubling news to contend with. Through his telescope he could now see the Prussian army approaching on his right and to his rear. Around 30,000 men of the Prussian IV Corps,

commanded by Friedrich Wilhelm Freiherr von Bülow, were advancing on the village of Plancenoit. If they could take this position, it would spell disaster for the French.

Spotting the threat, Napoleon committed ten battalions (around 6,000 men) of his Imperial Guard to help defend Plancenoit. These elite infantry reserves were a formidable opponent, and the fight for the village turned into a bloody struggle that lasted into the evening.

With the Prussian army outflanking him and Wellington's battered infantry seemingly holding firm, the battle was all but lost for the emperor. Determined, and perhaps desperate, he nonetheless made one last bid for victory, ordering his remaining elite Imperial Guard to advance on Mont-Saint-Jean.

By 6pm, the French had finally captured La Haye Sainte, which was a huge blow to

Wellington. Despite the arrival of his ally on the battlefield, the duke knew his men were close to breaking point.

Low on ammunition and with scores of casualties, the Anglo-Allied lines nonetheless formed ranks one last time to defend against the Imperial Guard. Dutch, Belgian and British volley fire at close range devastated the French, who advanced in square formation to protect against cavalry. A cry of "La garde recule!" ("The guard retreats!") went up as the guardsmen hastily withdrew.

By the late evening the French were in full retreat, and before the end of the month Napoleon had abdicated his throne. Wellington and Blücher greeted one another on the battlefield that evening. Wellington would later refer to the battle as "the nearest run thing you ever saw in your life".

"AT ONE POINT FRENCH SOLDIERS BROKE IN THROUGH THE NORTH GATE"

An illustration of the farmhouse of Hougoumont, which was defended by men of the Coldstream Guards and Nassau regiments

ARTHUR WELLESLEY, DUKE OF WELLINGTON

The third son of an Irish nobleman from County Meath, Arthur Wellesley was born in Ireland in 1769. After moving to England, Wellesley attended school in London then went to Eton College. In 1787 his elder brother, the earl of Mornington, bought him an officer's commission in the British Army, and he departed to serve in India. Largely through his family's influence, Wellesley purchased several quick promotions through the ranks and by 1793 was lieutenant-colonel of his own regiment. After service in Holland and India he was given command of the British expeditionary force to Portugal and Spain. It was during this period that Wellesley achieved many of his greatest victories, and for his success he was made duke of Wellington. After Waterloo he served twice as Prime Minister before his death in 1852.

The duke, painted 1815–16 by Thomas Lawrence), wearing his Field Marshal's uniform

Image Source • Apsley House

14:00–14:45
BRITISH CAVALRY CHARGES
Seeing an opportunity, the British Union and Household Brigades charge the French line, capturing two regimental eagles in the assault as their horses smash into French infantry.

16:00–18:00
FRENCH CAVALRY CHARGES
After repulsing the charge, over 4,500 French heavy cavalry gather to counter-attack. They charge over the ridgeline and into British infantry arrange in square formation.

16:00–21:00
PRUSSIANS ATTACK PLANCENOIT
Arriving to the rear and right of the French formation, Prussian infantry assault the French garrison in the village of Plancenoit – horrific close-quarters combat ensues.

18:30
THE FRENCH CAPTURE LA HAYE SAINTE
After hours of brutal fighting, the farmhouse of La Haye Sainte in the centre of Wellington's line is finally captured by French infantry, dealing a serious blow to the Duke's hopes of victory.

20:00
NAPOLEON IS DEFEATED
A final desperate attack by the French Imperial Guard is repulsed by merciless British volley fire. The elite troops withdraw and soon Napoleon's army is in full retreat, the emperor's dreams of triumph crushed.

THE BATTLEFIELD

THE BATTLE OF WATERLOO TOOK PLACE
WITHIN RAIN-SOAKED CROP FIELDS
AND FARMHOUSES

Image Source • Alamy

The 28th Regiment at
the Battle of Quatre Bas,
two days before the
Battle of Waterloo

WELLINGTON'S DEPLOYMENT
The Anglo-Allied army holds
three farm houses: Hougoumont,
La Haye Sainte and Papelotte.
A majority of the infantry are
situated atop an elevated ridge.

FRENCH CAVALRY CHARGE
Armed with swords and lances and
heavily armoured, Napoleon's cavalry
is successful against their British
counterparts but is unable to break
Wellington's infantry formations.

INFANTRY SQUARES
When facing French cavalry
charges, Wellington's infantry
forms tight ranks of
elongated squares, presenting
musket fire and bayonets to
prevent the units being
outflanked and scattered.

THE HOUGOUMONT FARMHOUSE

Napoleon's first objective is to take the small compound at Hougoumont. Lightly defended by only a few allied companies, a mass infantry attack is repulsed just as the men in the courtyard near breaking point.

THE DIVERSION BECOMES A MASS BATTLE

The French army is determined to take Hougoumont, believing that if they do Wellington's reserves will be drawn towards it and leave his centre exposed. Napoleon's eager brother Jérôme commands the attack on the farmhouse.

COALITION CAVALRY RESPONSE

Now low on reinforcements and thinly spread, the road to Brussels is opening, but as the coalition infantry stumble a cavalry charge rescues them.

D'ERLON'S ADVANCE

After the artillery barrage, Napoleon sends in his infantry. 17–20,000 Frenchmen led by d'Erlon rush into La Haye Sainte as the defenders, including members of the 95th Rifles and King's German Legion, are forced back.

RESOLUTE COALITION DEFENCE

The two-metre (six-foot) wall that surrounds the compound is stubbornly defended by the British, who fire their muskets and rifles through any gaps in the wall they can find. They hold out despite waves of French attacks.

THE MAIN ASSAULT

The Grande Batterie lines up in the middle of the field and fires countless bursts of round shots. The bombardment lasts for two hours and the allied lines are peppered with cannon shot.

THE PRUSSIANS ARRIVE

With the arrival of the Prussian army on his right flank, Napoleon sends his Imperial Guard to break Wellington's line – they fail and the battle is lost.

Image Source • Alamy

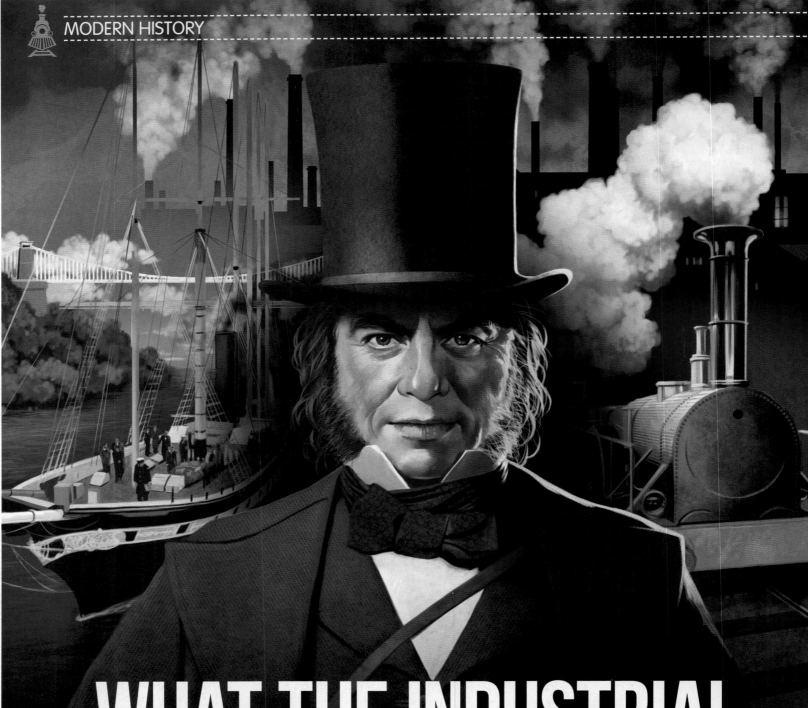

Image Source • Joe Cummings

WHAT THE INDUSTRIAL REVOLUTION DID FOR US

DELVE INTO THE ERA OF ENDLESS INVENTION, INNOVATION AND DISCOVERY THAT SHAPED
THE MODERN WORLD

Words by **Jodie Tyley and Tim Williamson**

Everything from selfies to sound systems, and iMacs to milkshakes owe their existence to the scientists and engineers of the 19th century. Motorcars, steam trains and even the humble bicycle enabled people to travel across vast distances quickly and cheaply for the first time. Studies of microbiology enhanced our understanding of diseases, leading the way to cures and immunisation, while the telephone, radio and telegraph revolutionised the way we communicate, connecting people across countries and continents. Here are just a few of the most important inventions and discoveries for which we can thank the geniuses of the Victorian age.

1817-1880S
BICYCLES

Although there are designs for two- and four-wheeled human-powered vehicles dating back all the way to the 15th century, the first successful, safe and popular human-powered bikes did not begin to emerge until some 400 years later. In 1817, German aristocrat Karl von Drais designed the Laufmaschine ('running machine'), which was simply two wheels on a wooden frame and a seat. To propel the machine the rider would simply run on the ground, then raise their feet and let the wheels do the work. By the 1860s a pedalled bicycle, called the velocipede, had been developed in France, which enabled riders to rotate the front wheel by foot. This was also known as the 'boneshaker' due to the uncomfortable ride caused by its solid wheels. By the 1880s the modern bike had taken shape, with the pedals moved to the centre of the frame, powering the rear wheel via a chain to enable greater control and stability.

RIGHT The Rover safety bicycle was far safer and more stable than previous bikes and formed the blueprint for future designs

Image Source • Getty

1865
PASTEURISATION

Before the mid 19th century, food and drink had an incredibly short shelf life –in particular milk deteriorated very quickly, becoming foul smelling, undrinkable and wasted. This changed with the development of pasteurisation, a process of heating liquid until almost boiling to destroy as many harmful microorganisms as possible before rapidly cooling it. Chemist Louis Pasteur made his discovery while researching the fermentation process of wine. He was attempting to discover the cause of sour or spoiled wine and found that the rapid heating and cooling prevented any germs or microbes causing contamination. His studies also created a greater understanding of the role of living microorganisms during fermentation. The Frenchman lent his name to his discovery, which today is a vital stage in the mass production of dairy and alcohol products. However, his research into microbiology, or germ theory, also led to a greater understanding of the causes of and cures for diseases.

Image Source • Alamy

Louis Pasteur was one of the 19th century's leading microbiologists

An engraving showing the deadly pollution of the Thames

Image Source • Getty

1866
LONDON'S SEWER SYSTEM

In the early 19th century, the River Thames was a stinking cesspit of raw sewage. Disease was rife and more than 10,000 Londoners were killed by cholera between 1853 and 1854. One particularly hot summer brought the city to a standstill in what was called the 'Great Stink', finally prompting the government to take action. Chief engineer Joseph Bazalgette constructed an underground network of intercepting sewers that collected the waste that flowed out to the Thames using gravity and the occasional huge steam pump. The sewers were dug by hand – mechanical diggers didn't exist – and constructed using 318 million bricks and new water-resistant Portland cement. However, the sewage still wasn't 'treated' until the 1880s!

1866
STEPHENSON'S ROCKET

Among the first major steps on track to steam-powered passenger trains came in 1829 when engineers George and Robert Stephenson's 'Rocket' reached a top speed of 48 kilometres (29 miles) per hour – a lightning pace for the era. Although it wasn't the very first steam locomotive, Rocket combined several efficient design features and was selected to service on one of the world's first passenger railway lines, the Liverpool and Manchester Railway.

CYLINDERS
Two angled cylinders were positioned on each side of Rocket. Each contained a piston and were connected to the wheels via cranks.

BOILER
Rocket's boiler was heated by multiple copper tubes, which ran from the firebox. These enabled heat to be transferred very efficiently.

PISTON
The change in pressure created by the build-up of steam drove the piston back and forth, which in turn drove Rocket's wheels.

BLAST PIPE
Steam from the boiler moved up through a blastpipe and into the cylinder, where the pressure would build.

Illustration • The Art Agency/Nick Sellers

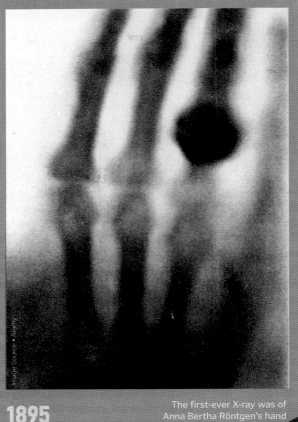

Image Source • Alamy

1895
X-RAYS

The first-ever X-ray was of Anna Bertha Röntgen's hand

One of the 19th century's most important discoveries happened entirely by accident. German physicist Wilhelm Conrad Röntgen was experimenting with passing electrical currents through gas-filled tubes, similar to fluorescent light bulbs when he noticed a screen start to glow. It was illuminated by invisible rays coming from a tube that was covered in black paper, meaning they had the power to penetrate solid objects! Röntgen created the first X-ray image by swapping the screen for a photographic plate. The image revealed the bones in his wife's hand. The rays passed through tissue easier than bone, and the 'shadows' this creates form an image. X-rays are a type of high-frequency electromagnetic radiation similar to light but, unlike light, their higher energy means they can pass through most objects.

1877
PHONOGRAPH

A cross between the telephone and telegraph, this unusual contraption could both record sound and play it back. Its inventor, Thomas Edison, envisioned it being used for dictating letters, for recording lessons in school or recording phone conversations, to name a few applications. The first words he recorded were "Mary had a little lamb" and he was amazed when the machine played his words back.

RIGHT Thomas Edison seated next to his invention in 1878

Image Source • Alamy

REPRODUCER SOUND BOX
The recording on the tinfoil vibrated the needle (stylus), which in turn vibrated the diaphragm, reproducing the original sound.

RECOIL
A stylus on the other side would be placed into the groove and the cylinder was put in its original position.

HAND CRANK
This turned the cylinder that was wrapped in tinfoil.

RECORDING STYLUS
A needle called a stylus moved with the vibrations from the diaphragm, making indentations on the tinfoil cylinder in vertical grooves.

RECORDING SOUND BOX
The user would speak into this, directing sound waves into the diaphragm – a thin membrane that vibrated.

Image Source • Alamy

AN AGE OF PROGRESS

1839
Light-sensitive photographic paper
William Henry Fox Talbot
By using light-sensitive silver nitrate, Talbot created 'photogenic drawings'.

1843
Christmas card
Sir Henry Cole
Henry Cole was too busy to write to his friends over the holiday season, so commissioned the first Christmas card.

Image • John Calicott Horsley

1846
Sewing machine
Elias Howe
This was not the first sewing machine, but Howe's refined design has much more in common with our modern machines.

1849
First glider to be flown by a pilot
George Cayley
A replica on display at the Yorkshire Air Museum.

Image • Nigel Coates

Image • William Henry Fox Talbot

1840
Adhesive postage stamp
Sir Rowland Hill
Joseph Lister is born in Upton, Essex, to Quaker parents Isabella Harris and Joseph Jackson Lister, the fourth of their seven children.

1844
Morse Code
Samuel Morse

1845
Rubber tyres
Robert Thomson

Image • Scientific American magazine

1848
Modern water turbine
James Francis

1849
Concrete
Joseph Monier

1851
Public flushing toilets
George Jennings

THE EVOLUTION OF PHOTOGRAPHY

A snapshot of cameras through time

1685 CAMERA OBSCURA

1841 VOIGTLANDER AGUERREOTYPE CAMERA

1888 ORIGINAL KODAK CAMERA

1900 KODAK BROWNIE

1925 LEICA

1929 ROLLEIFLEX

1937 MINOX SUB-MINIATURE CAMERA

1949 CANON IIB

1959 OLYMPUS PEN FIRST-GENERATION

1963 KODAK INSTAMATIC 50

1972 POLAROID SX-70

1876 TELEPHONE

The first words ever spoken on the telephone were: "Mr Watson, come here; I want to see you." It was inventor Alexander Graham Bell talking to his assistant on 10 March 1876. The telephone he created looked very different to its modern counterparts, but operated using a mouthpiece, transmitter and a receiver.

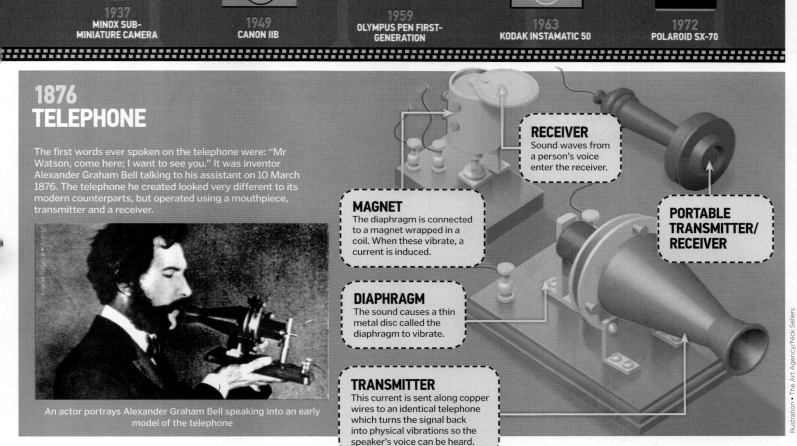

An actor portrays Alexander Graham Bell speaking into an early model of the telephone

RECEIVER
Sound waves from a person's voice enter the receiver.

MAGNET
The diaphragm is connected to a magnet wrapped in a coil. When these vibrate, a current is induced.

PORTABLE TRANSMITTER/RECEIVER

DIAPHRAGM
The sound causes a thin metal disc called the diaphragm to vibrate.

TRANSMITTER
This current is sent along copper wires to an identical telephone which turns the signal back into physical vibrations so the speaker's voice can be heard.

Illustration • The Art Agency/Nick Sellers

1853
Post box
Richard Redgrave
The unusual octagonal design was made by John M Butt & Co of Gloucester, England.

1863
Underground railway
London's Metropolitan Railway opened between Paddington and Farringdon Street.

Image • George Iles

1873
Denim jeans
Jacob Davis and Levi Strauss

1885
Three-wheeled motor car 'motorwagen'
Karl Benz

1863
Underground railway
London's Metropolitan Railway opened between Paddington and Farringdon Street.

1895
Wireless communication
Guglielmo Marconi

Image • Felix O

1854
Turning iron into steel
Henry Bessemer

Image • Wiki; author unknown.

1873
Typewriter
Christopher Sholes
The first commercially successful typewriter included the QWERTY keyboard.

1879
Electric light bulb
Thomas Edison
He wasn't the first to develop the light bulb, but Edison improved the design so it lasted longer.

Image • Getty

Image • Jaybear

1895
Cinematograph
Lumière brothers
This motion picture film camera also doubled as a projector.

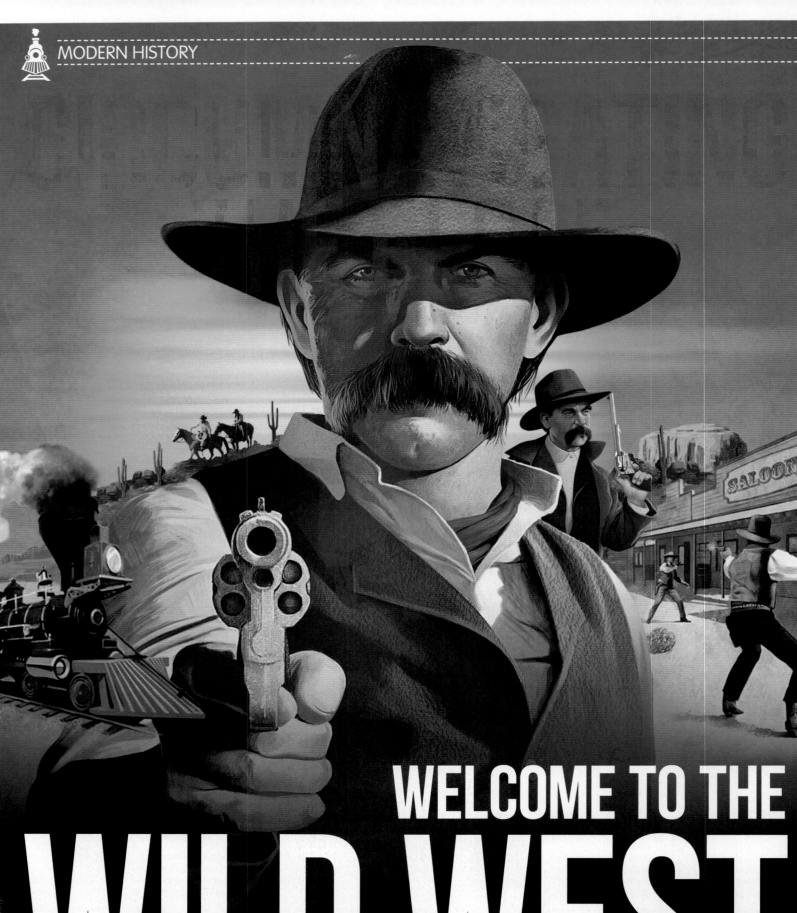

WELCOME TO THE
WILD WEST

VISIT THE HARSH LANDS OF THE OLD WEST AND THE PEOPLE WHO CALLED IT HOME

The discovery of precious metals attracted large numbers of miners to the west

WILD WEST MYTHS BUSTED

Everyone was an outlaw
There are probably more iconic criminals from this brief period of history than any other, but most settlers in the west were simple farmers and miners.

Cowboys were gunslingers
Although the term is often used to describe a pistol-wielding mercenary, a 'cowboy' was a farmer who herded and tended to cattle, mostly while on horseback.

Saloons were dangerous places
This is only part myth, as saloons were certainly fatal for many customers. But they also served as town halls on occasion, and some respected lawmen owned their own establishments.

Whisky was the drink of choice
Although it was called whisky, the alcohol served in saloons was more akin to a modern moonshine – it was typically a combination of raw alcohol, burnt sugar and chewing tobacco.

Guns were everywhere
The early Wild West was dangerous, but as time wore on and towns became safer, carrying a gun became unnecessary. Some settlements even banned them from being carried.

When we picture the Wild West, we immediately think of a scorched desert where cowboys, sheriffs and bandits shelter from the Sun in saloons with swinging doors. There they sit drinking whisky and eyeing each other suspiciously, their twitching fingers hovering by the revolver pistol strapped to their waist, all ready for a mass gunfight at a moment's notice.

So how accurate is this Hollywood depiction of the Old West? And how did this fascinating period of history arise? In this feature, we're going to step into a pair of spurred riding boots and head into the sandy towns of western America during the mid 19th century. But first we'll explore how the first settlers arrived there.

By 1790 the United States of America had been born. The former 13 British colonies on the east coast had unified, and the colonists soon turned their attention westward towards the rest of the unexplored North American continent. These settlers had paid a bloody price for their independence from Britain, and in their pursuit of new conquest, territory and ownership would find much more violence in the years to come.

Fast forward to the 1840s and the colonists had successfully navigated their way from territory to territory and arrived on the western coast. They had ousted the Native American and Mexican inhabitants and begun to make themselves at home. They were then followed by a surge of new settlers in 1848 when gold was discovered in the Californian region. The influx of people quickly outpaced the sophistication of the towns that housed them, and the new settlements became unruly places. The era of the Wild West had begun.

Movies and literature are saturated with stories of gunslingers – pistol-wielding 'cowboys' who blew bandits away with their quick-draw techniques, but most inhabitants of the West were at first miners and farmers. The government even gave away land for free to settlers who opted to migrate west, permitted they remained for several years. But some inevitably fell on hard times – in part due to the unforgiving soil – and opted to embrace the life of an outlaw. Criminal numbers grew in the following years when the American Civil War ended and guerrilla fighters on the losing side sought plunder instead of farmland.

The turbulent new country of the US became host to a western frontier that was dominated by quests of expansion and conquest but was famed for robberies and banditry, gunslingers and law enforcers. It was an exceptional time, and within these pages we can learn more about this fascinating period. Are you ready, gunslinger?

"THE TURBULENT WESTERN FRONTIER BECAME FAMED FOR ROBBERIES AND BANDITRY"

The new railways helped to unify the west with the rest of the country

LAW AND ORDER IN THE OLD WEST

HOW SHERIFFS, BOUNTY HUNTERS AND TOURING JUDGES DELIVERED JUSTICE TO THE WESTERN FRONTIER

If the Second Amendment of the US Constitution – which describes the right of the people to bear arms – teaches us anything, it's that American citizens spent a large period of their history without established law enforcement. This was especially prevalent in the Old West, where the colonists were mostly left to take the law into their own hands, and their ability to play the role of judge, jury and executioner led to a unique and dangerous form of justice.

When colonists first endured the gruelling journey to the western regions and discovered the potential treasures to be had there, the new towns and settlements soon saw their numbers swell. A town originally populated purely by prospectors and farmers swiftly became home to large numbers of new miners and traders.

The rate of crime inevitably soared with the booming population and theft, saloon brawls

Gambling, especially while playing the card game *Faro*, was popular in saloons

Image Source • Getty

and gunfights all became more common. In the absence of a structured law system many territory settlements passed judgements themselves and corruption was rife. It seemed that the rule and procedure of law also had to make the slow migration to the west coast.

Eventually, the more established colonies hired sheriffs and marshals to keep the peace. These men would lock up drunkards and aggressors and track down more notorious outlaws with the help of citizens. To attract these bounty hunters the lawmen used 'Wanted' posters, which promised a handsome reward for a fugitive captured 'dead or alive'. Famous outlaws were worth huge amounts – Jesse James, for example, was worth $5,000, which was a considerable sum for the time.

If taken alive, the captured parties were sometimes placed in front of touring judges that had come from neighbouring regions to deliver justice. These officials were quite different to the judges of today, preferring to hold court in an informal fashion. Resting their feet on a desk, whittling and chewing tobacco were all acceptable behaviours for a presiding lawman. And the bizarre practices didn't end there. On the western frontier, where money was scarce, wealthy parties were often fined if convicted of a crime. And on at least one occasion the guilty party paid in warm clothing for the judge and marshal! Even more so than today, money and violence ruled in the Wild West.

> ## "MONEY AND VIOLENCE RULED IN THE WILD WEST"

TOWN HERO

ABIGAIL SCOTT DUNIWAY

Not every hero of the Wild West was a rambunctious gunslinger, as Abigail Scott Duniway proved during her remarkable lifetime. Crossing into Oregon in 1852, Duniway was hired as a schoolteacher but later found her calling as a champion for women's rights. At the age of 78 she became the first woman to vote in her county.

TOWN HERO

WYATT EARP

The line between noble lawmen and opportunistic mercenary was a blurry one in the Old West, but Wyatt Earp is largely celebrated as a great law enforcer in a region that really needed it. Described as "absolutely destitute of physical fear", Earp excelled as a policeman, assistant city marshal and stagecoach guard during his career.

KEY DATES IN THE HISTORY OF THE WILD WEST

1820s
Colonist 'mountain men' travel west to the Rockies for hunting.

1841
A wagon train makes the first journey to the northwest coast.

1844
1,500 settlers migrate from the eastern territories and arrive in California.

1846
The US declares war on Mexico, which claims ownership of the west.

1848
Mexico concedes and agrees to sell California and its northern territories.

TOWN HERO

ANNIE OAKLEY

Born under the name Phoebe Moses, the woman who became Annie Oakley gained fame as a sharpshooter through Buffalo Bill's Wild West shows. Oakley was so accurate with her rifle that she could shoot the ash off the tip of a cigarette! Native American Chief Sitting Bull gifted her a worthy nickname: 'Little Sure Shot'.

HEROES AND VILLAINS
Meet the exceptional characters who epitomised life in the Old West

WANTED

BELLE STARR

Starr gained such infamy during her lifetime that most tales of her exploits have now been distorted by fiction. After the civil war we know she allied herself with guerrilla groups who specialised in robbing banks, stagecoaches and fellow settlers. For years she planned crimes, harboured fugitives and committed robberies before meeting a grisly end.

WANTED

DOC HOLLIDAY

Before turning to a wild life, John Henry 'Doc' Holliday was a practising dentist. He decided to travel to the drier climate in the west to alleviate a chronic cough and soon found himself entangled in numerous gunfights. He later took up a life of gambling and was suspected of robbery and murder.

WANTED

BUTCH CASSIDY & THE SUNDANCE KID

Robert Parker (Butch Cassidy) and Harry Longabaugh (The Sundance Kid) helped to form the Wild Bunch, a group of former labourers who turned to crime in search of bigger profits. For years they succeeded in robbing banks and trains, retreating to the deep canyons of Wyoming and Utah to hide from the law after a heist.

WANTED

BLACK BART

Charles Boles was a California stagecoach robber who garnered a reputation for being incredibly well mannered and polite to his victims. He acquired his villainous identity from a 'dime novel' in a local newspaper in which a man with black hair, a black beard and black clothes robbed unsuspecting stagecoaches. His name was Black Bart.

WANTED

BILLY THE KID

Born Henry McCarty in New York City, Billy the Kid came to the fore on the other side of the country in New Mexico, where his notorious criminal career began. He shot and killed someone in a saloon fight and joined a faction war while still an adolescent. After committing a series of murders he was killed himself, aged just 21.

Illustrations • Adam Markiewicz

1848
Prospectors discover gold near Sacramento for the first time.

1849
40,000 gold miners arrive in the west, starting the famous California Gold Rush.

1850
Native Americans of the Sierra Nevada fight the prospectors.

1850
Home to over 60,000, California becomes the 31st US state.

LIFE IN A WILD WEST TOWN

HOW SHERIFFS, BOUNTY HUNTERS AND TOURING JUDGES
DELIVERED JUSTICE TO THE WESTERN FRONTIER

Image Source • L. C. McClure

SALOONS

After a hard day's work, there was little settlers enjoyed more than visiting the saloon. It was home to all manner of debauchery, including dancing girls, hard liquor, gambling and sometimes even gunfights. Early saloons were little more than tents propped up on the roadside in the hopes of luring in a weary traveller, but as towns grew they transformed into something more like the swinging-door establishments we're all familiar with.

Saloons were popular places where settlers could drink liquor, play card games and gamble

JOBS

The famous California Gold Rush and other subsequent precious metal finds brought miners and prospectors to the west in their thousands. And where people go, trade follows; soon bartenders, merchants, doctors and entertainers all arrived in the region. The government encouraged this migration and offered free farmland to new settlers, which helped develop the western economy further and paved the way for more investment and more job opportunities in the region.

Most settlers in the Old West's early years worked as miners and prospectors

Image Source • Getty

TRAVEL

The first colonists to arrive in the west did so the old-fashioned way. Aside from their animal helpers to carry their supplies, and them on occasion, it was traversing terrain on foot that carried them to their new lives. Wagon trains were especially popular – chains of large, horse-drawn vehicles that carried large amounts of goods. Railways began to arrive not long after as the government offered free land to rail companies if they agreed to place track westwards.

To most, trains were a revolutionary way to travel. To others, they were a target

Image Source • Getty

"MOST GUNFIGHTS WERE FOUGHT BEHIND COVER BETWEEN GROUPS OF INTOXICATED MEN"

1853
Washington is organised as a territory to support new colonists.

1860
The James Gang begins its notorious career of robbing trains, stagecoaches and banks.

1862
The Homestead Act offers free western farming land, permitted the settlers stay for five years.

1865
The American Civil War comes to an end. Some guerrilla soldiers become criminals in the west.

1865
The editor of the *New York Tribune* advises readers: "Go West, young man."

INFRASTRUCTURE

The first settlers of the Old West would have loved the things we take for granted, like access to unlimited clean water and a grocery store. When they first arrived at the frontier they stored water taken from springs and they hunted and foraged for food and skins. Later they graduated to digging wells and forming crop and animal farms. Timber-framed homes followed, then the first giant distilleries were built to create precious, low-quality whiskey.

The western frontier was typically dry and arid, making access to clean water essential

ENTERTAINMENT

As fun as bounty hunting, duelling and simply firing a six-shooter must have been, most settlers had to find other means of entertainment in the Old West. Saloons were incredibly popular, and newspapers and 'dime novels' were widely read. In later years, travelling actors also toured the towns putting on shows, and homegrown entertainers soon began to appear.

Dime novels were incredibly popular in the Old West and inspired many future stories of the era

"EARLY SALOONS WERE LITTLE MORE THAN TENTS"

GUNFIGHTS

Our romanticised idea of civilised duels in the Wild West are in truth quite far from the mark. Although single duels did happen rarely, the Hollywood depiction of two men stood facing each other in an empty street has its origins in 19th-century dime novels rather than actual historical records.

Most gunfights were actually fought behind cover between groups of intoxicated men – there are many recorded examples of gamblers using guns to resolve a card game dispute!

Quick-draw duels were an invention of 19th-century literature and rarely happened in reality

COMMUNICATION

Some colonists travelled hundreds if not thousands of miles westwards to find work or claim land in the new territories. However, thanks to the invention of the telegraph in 1831, there was a much faster way of communicating with those left behind than simply sending a letter. Settlers could have their messages translated into Morse code and sent through electrical wires that connected to a distant station. This could then be decoded on the other side, resulting in an incredibly quick messaging method.

Before the telegraph, the Pony Express was used to deliver mail between the east and west of the US

1869
The US's first transcontinental railway running across the country is completed.

1881
Lawmen and ranchers clash over a silver mine at the OK Corral.

1883
Buffalo Bill Cody starts touring with his Wild West show.

1890
Idaho and Wyoming are admitted to the Union, becoming the 43rd and 44th states.

1907
The state of Oklahoma is created by combining the Indian and Oklahoma Territories.

1916
The last stage robbery of the Old West takes place in Jarbridge Canyon, Nevada.

ANATOMY OF A 19TH CENTURY FIREMAN

HOW THE USA'S VOLUNTEERS PUT THE FIGHT IN FIREFIGHTER

Today, firefighters are brave heroes that come to our rescue with efficiency and professionalism, but that hasn't always been the case. During the late 18th century and early 19th century, firefighters in the USA didn't have such a good reputation. Rather than being employed by the government, they were typically volunteers who had been let off military service or jury duty, and had to buy their own uniforms and equipment.

Firehouses became like social clubs and when news of a fire broke, the volunteers would race those from other fire companies to reach the scene first, dragging heavy hand-operated water pumps with them. These competitions often resulted in the firefighters battling each other instead of the fire!

Soon, local gangs began associating themselves with the firehouses, and the firefighters became involved in party politics. This resulted in even more violence, with the firefighters sometimes starting fires themselves. One particularly lethal confrontation in 1856 became known as the Know-Nothing riot, and saw several people killed at Lexington Market in Baltimore.

By the mid 19th century, insurance companies and the Republican Party were lobbying for a professional fire service and when horse-drawn, steam-powered water pumps became available, the volunteers were replaced with paid fire departments.

HELMET
The reinforced dome helmets made from specially treated leather had an angled brim so that water could run off the back.

BEARD
Firefighters would soak their beards in water, bite them, then breathe through them to prevent themselves from inhaling fumes from the fire.

RED SHIRT
Bright red, bibbed shirts helped people identify the firefighters, and they soon became a symbol of elevated social status.

SPEAKING TRUMPET
Excited and noisy crowds would often come to watch the firefighters at work, so they used brass speaking trumpets to relay commands.

HOSE
The leather hose had seams held together by metal rivets to stop it rupturing under the pressure of the water.

LEATHER BOOTS
Knee-high leather boots were worn mainly to keep the firefighters warm and dry, rather than protect them from the flames.

FIGHTING FIRES BY HAND

Before steam-powered fire engines, firefighters used hand-operated pumps to douse fires with water. These machines on wheels would be pulled through the streets by horse or by the firefighters themselves. Some had to be filled by hand, with so-called 'bucket brigades' of local helpers fetching water from nearby sources, but others were equipped with a suction hose that could draw water directly from municipal hydrants.

The firefighters would then pump the long levers up and down to operate a set of pistons inside. The movement of the pistons would alternately suck water out of the main tank and force it into a separate chamber. The air trapped inside the chamber would maintain a constant pressure helping to spray the water out through a hose. It requires an exhausting 60 strokes per minute to pump the water effectively, so teams of firefighters would take turns to operate the machine for a few minutes at a time.

Main Illustration • Kevin McGivern

ON BOARD THE PULLMAN TRAIN

WHY WAS THE PULLMAN RAILWAY CARRIAGE FIT FOR A QUEEN?

The first half of the 19th century saw a rapid expansion in train travel. New companies and tracks sprang up in the wake of Britain's first steam railway, which opened on 15 September 1830 and linked the growing northern industrial cities of Liverpool and Manchester.

The Pullman Palace Car Company was established in 1862 in the United States. Although specialising in sleeper cars, which were more popular in America due to the greater distances, the company began exporting passenger coaches to Britain 1874.

Far from being late to the party, Pullman quickly cornered the market on luxury. Appealing to the growing middle classes who had money to treat themselves, Pullman coaches offered leather seats, table lamps, dining cars, attentive stewards serving food and drink, and even heating and air conditioning. With the agreement of its American counterpart, a British version – the Pullman Car Company – formed in 1882 to produce similar carriages from a workshop in Brighton.

The coaches and the service George Pullman would have recognised endured into the 1960s and 1970s, when classic Pullman coaches began to be replaced by designs fit for the age of diesel power and regular commuter travel. However, they are still used on heritage railways today. An instantly recognisable symbol of a lost era of elegance, Pullman coaches have been used by the royal family and have even survived bomb damage during World War II.

PULLMAN AND CIVIL RIGHTS

By the 1920s, the Pullman Palace Car Company had become one of the largest employers of African-Americans in the United States. However, conditions were still poor for black porters who relied on tips from passengers for income and were denied promotion to jobs specially reserved for white employees.

On 25 August 1925, the Brotherhood of Sleeping Car Porters (BSCP) was formed with the motto "Fight or Be Slaves", and after a long battle it became the first African-American trade union officially recognised by the American Federation of Labor in 1935.

Some BSCP members would later play key roles in the civil rights movement. Among the most famous members are co-founder Asa Philip Randolph, who organised Martin Luther King's 1963 March on Washington where he made his famous "I Have A Dream" speech, and Edgar Nixon, who organised the 1955 Montgomery Bus Boycott in response to the arrest of Rosa Parks for defying racist laws in the Deep South.

INSIDE THE COACH

Discover how the Pullman carriage got its reputation

LIVERY
From 1906, the colour scheme of the Pullman Car Company was umber and cream, with "Pullman" written in gold.

COMFORT
The fashionable art deco interior had electric table lamps, table clothes and upholstered seats.

FINE DINING
The dining car was open to both Standard and First Class passengers, but First Class got dibs.

ENGINE
The steam train itself was essentially a large boiler that produced steam with enough force to power its wheels.

COAL CAR
The tender, or coal car, often contained not just coal for the steam engine, but water and wood too.

LUGGAGE VAN
Luggage vans could carry either the passengers' belongings, or parcels and post for Royal Mail.

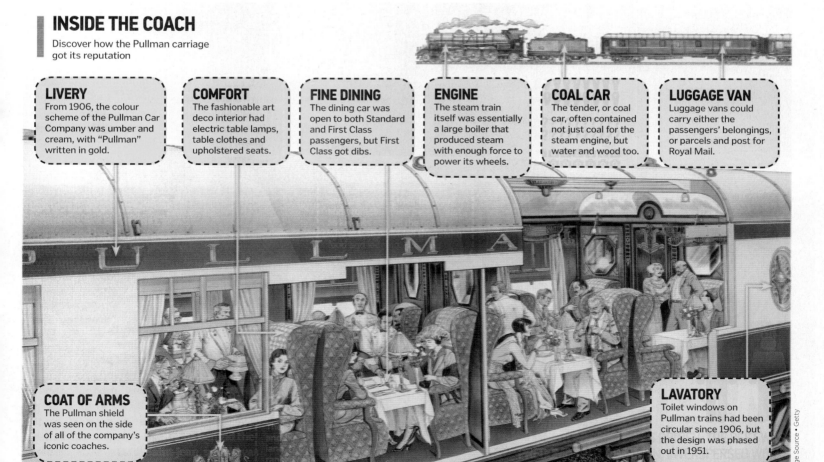

COAT OF ARMS
The Pullman shield was seen on the side of all of the company's iconic coaches.

LAVATORY
Toilet windows on Pullman trains had been circular since 1906, but the design was phased out in 1951.

Image Source • Getty

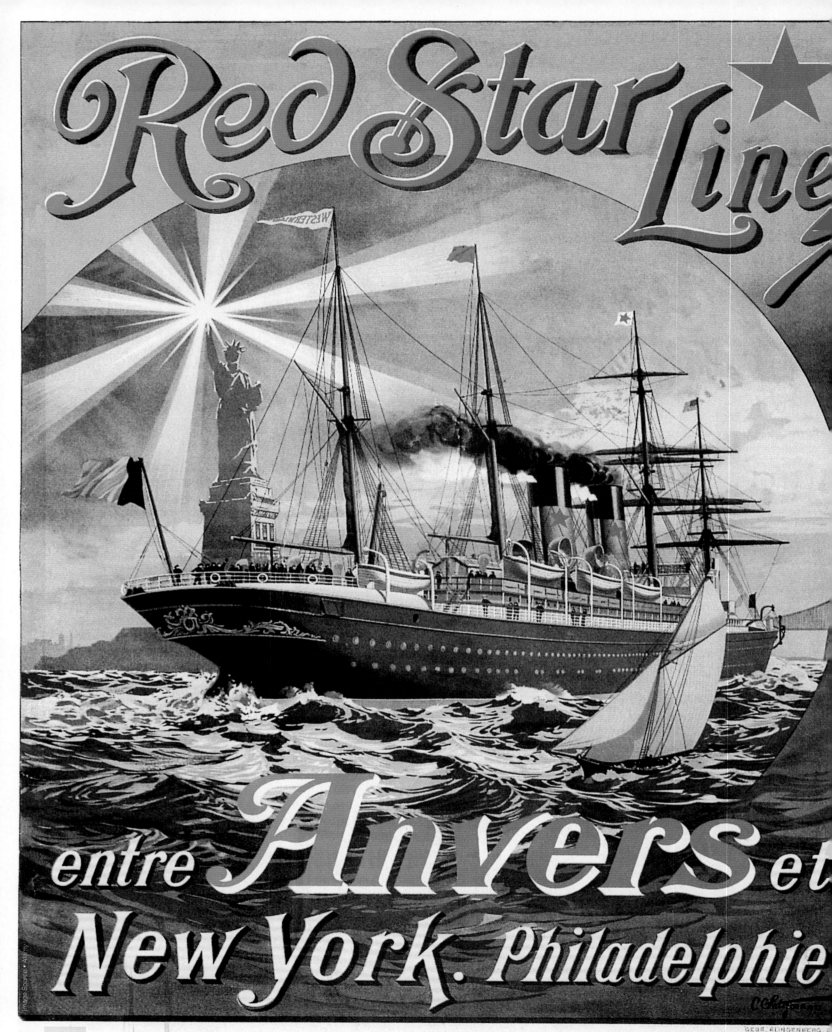

JOURNEY TO AMERICA

DURING THE 19TH CENTURY MILLIONS TRAVELLED TO SEEK FREEDOM AND FORTUNE IN THE US

Words by **Tim Williamson**

America, as former President John F Kennedy pointed out, is a nation of immigrants. Today, an overwhelming majority of Americans, from Donald Trump to Kim Kardashian, can find immigrant blood not too far back in their family tree. Some of these ancestors arrived seeking to make their fortune in business or trade, or to find a better quality of life. However, others made the long journey to escape persecution, poverty and even genocide in their land of birth. Towards the end of the 19th century, both these factors led to a huge rise in immigration to the United States.

150 years ago there seemed no better prospect than the opportunities and freedoms available in the United States. After the end of the Civil War in 1865 the country underwent massive restoration, continuing its industrialisation and expansion to the west. Before long it was already surpassing the UK as the world's leading industrial power. The bustling factories and busy dockyards in cities such as New York, Baltimore, Boston and Philadelphia were huge draws for migrants seeking work.

These cities became key destinations for the major transatlantic ferry routes, which in the new age of steam were transporting more people across the ocean, and quicker than ever before. Records for the fastest crossing were smashed almost every year, and rival shipping companies were in constant competition to build the fastest ships. This meant passengers travelling from Italy, Ireland, Germany, the UK and elsewhere could make the journey across the Atlantic in a few days rather than the gruelling ordeal of a few weeks. This fierce competition sometimes resulted in tragedy, such as the sinking of RMS Titanic in 1912.

Catastrophic accidents aside, travelling aboard the liners was a pleasant cruise for first- and second-class passengers, while life for the majority in third class, or steerage, was far less pleasant. These were the cheapest tickets and afforded only cramped living space, with little or no access to the open air on deck. Almost all steerage passengers were migrants from among the poorest of society, and the deck would be filled with accents spanning from the Mediterranean to the Baltic Sea.

Regardless of what they had left behind, for most immigrants the first sight of their new home was the Statue of Liberty in New York Harbor, at the time a shimmering light brown colour rather than the green we see today. A plaque on the base of the monument reads, "Give us your tired, your poor, your huddled masses yearning to breathe free". It was a welcome to the New World to those travelling from the old.

The largest group to enter the United States between 1880 and 1920 were Italians. Approximately 4 million arrived during this period, a large proportion of whom were men seeking work either in order to settle or to send money back home. In fact, many of those arriving in the States did not look to stay permanently, but hoped to earn a decent wage and then return home. Millions of lira (the old Italian currency) were sent back to the old country by those working in America, helping to support their families.

At the beginning of the 20th century, there

A ferry carrying immigrants docks at Ellis Island, circa 1902-13
Image Source • New York Public Library

Image Source • Alamy

An inspection card issued to a migrant arriving at Ellis Island in 1925

IMMIGRATION BY NUMBERS: 1890–1919
Where did the majority of immigrants come from?

GERMANY 1,082,021

IRELAND 917,095

UK 1,170,155

RUSSIA 3,058,400

AUSTRIA-HUNGARY 3,690,162

ITALY 3,764,152

were already large Italian-American communities in major American cities, making it easier for new immigrants to settle. In 1900, New York's Italian population numbered 225,000 – a small but significant minority in a city of 3.4 million. New arrivals would usually know family members or friends already living within these communities who could help them find work and a place to stay.

Other nationalities and groups were not as well established during this period. From the 1880s, Jews living in the Russian Empire faced increased discrimination and were targeted with violence and oppressive laws. Although Jews made up only five per cent of the Russian population at the time, they accounted for 50 per cent of the country's immigrants to the United States. Many of them arrived with experience as merchants, tailors and peddlers, bringing with them a range of skills.

America's large cities were already home to large Jewish communities of several nationalities, and the new arrivals from Eastern Europe were able to easily settle in these neighbourhoods, particularly in New York's 'Little Germany' in Lower Manhattan. This nickname was rather misleading, as the area was also home to many Lithuanians, Poles, Ukrainians, Austrians and others. Here, successful second-generation Jewish families were gradually moving out to the expanding suburbs at the city limits, leaving room for others to settle and find their piece of the American Dream.

However, not all Americans were welcoming to what became known as the 'new immigrants', as opposed to first-, second- or even third-generation immigrants from previous decades. In 1892, Ellis Island opened in New York Harbor as the new official facility through which immigrants entering New York would be processed and assessed.

The rules governing those who would and would not be permitted entry became stricter as time went by, with subsequent laws piling on to stop would-be citizens. At first, only those with

infectious diseases were sent home or quarantined, then known criminals, then anyone deemed to be "mentally deficient" or "feeble-minded". People were put through often humiliating medical and mental tests to determine whether they were likely to become a burden on society, but relatively few were actually deported as a result.

By the late 1920s, immigration numbers were beginning to fall, before the Great Depression crippled the economy and jobs disappeared. Suddenly it seemed the land of prosperity was no longer the dream many had hoped for. The economic downturn would not last, but immigration numbers would never reach the same highs of previous decades. Nevertheless, the impact and importance of these immigrants-turned-citizens is still apparent today in their descendants.

Immigrants on Ellis Island awaiting inspection

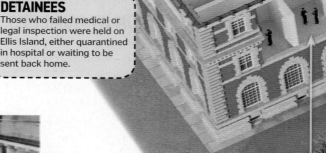

ELLIS ISLAND
For over 12 million people, this facility was the gateway to the United States

FINAL STEPS
Once the final inspection was complete, passengers were free to exchange their money into dollars and buy a train ticket to their next destination, and their new lives.

REGISTRY ROOM
This large hall was lined with a maze of rails, which formed passengers into orderly lines while they waited for medical and legal inspection.

DETAINEES
Those who failed medical or legal inspection were held on Ellis Island, either quarantined in hospital or waiting to be sent back home.

PAPERS, PLEASE
Immigration officials checked passengers' documents and asked a series of questions to verify their identity. Any persons judged to be suspicious were detained.

Image Source • Alamy

Illustration • Nicholas Forder

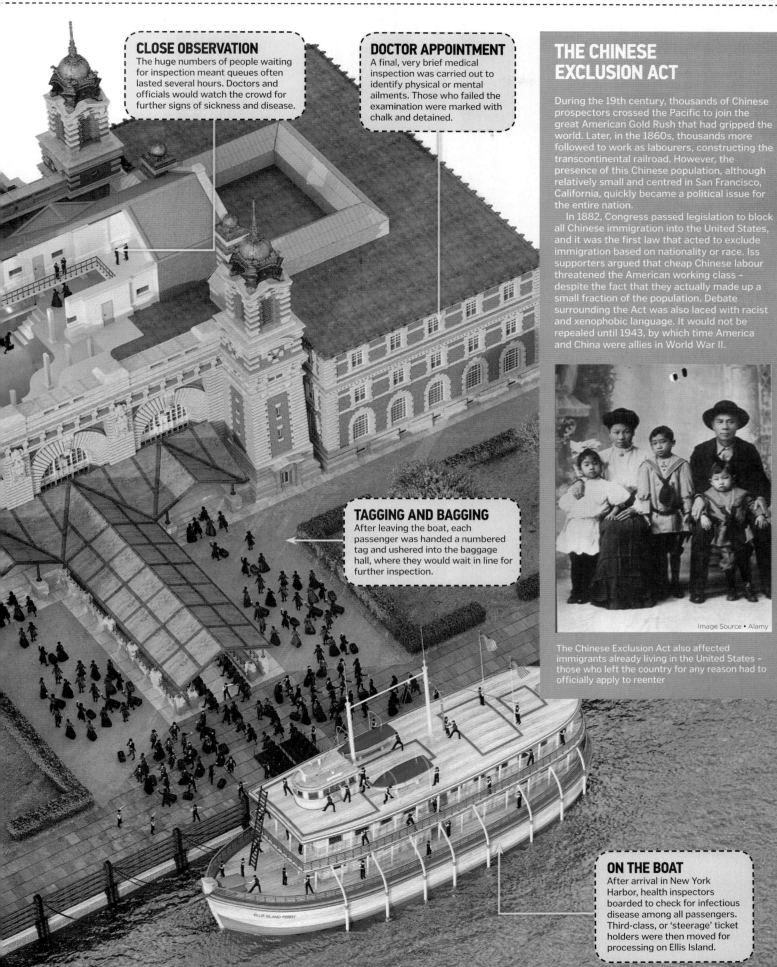

CLOSE OBSERVATION
The huge numbers of people waiting for inspection meant queues often lasted several hours. Doctors and officials would watch the crowd for further signs of sickness and disease.

DOCTOR APPOINTMENT
A final, very brief medical inspection was carried out to identify physical or mental ailments. Those who failed the examination were marked with chalk and detained.

TAGGING AND BAGGING
After leaving the boat, each passenger was handed a numbered tag and ushered into the baggage hall, where they would wait in line for further inspection.

ON THE BOAT
After arrival in New York Harbor, health inspectors boarded to check for infectious disease among all passengers. Third-class, or 'steerage' ticket holders were then moved for processing on Ellis Island.

THE CHINESE EXCLUSION ACT

During the 19th century, thousands of Chinese prospectors crossed the Pacific to join the great American Gold Rush that had gripped the world. Later, in the 1860s, thousands more followed to work as labourers, constructing the transcontinental railroad. However, the presence of this Chinese population, although relatively small and centred in San Francisco, California, quickly became a political issue for the entire nation.

In 1882, Congress passed legislation to block all Chinese immigration into the United States, and it was the first law that acted to exclude immigration based on nationality or race. Iss supporters argued that cheap Chinese labour threatened the American working class – despite the fact that they actually made up a small fraction of the population. Debate surrounding the Act was also laced with racist and xenophobic language. It would not be repealed until 1943, by which time America and China were allies in World War II.

Image Source • Alamy

The Chinese Exclusion Act also affected immigrants already living in the United States – those who left the country for any reason had to officially apply to reenter

THE 20TH CENTURY

100

124

THE MODEL T ASSEMBLY LINE

HENRY FORD'S PIONEERING MANUFACTURING PROCESS PUT THE WORLD ON WHEELS

Image Sources • The Ford Motor Company

Before Henry Ford opened the first moving assembly line on 7 October 1913 at the Highland Park Assembly plant in Michigan, car manufacturing was an incredibly slow and costly process. Ford's ambitious goal was to produce the highest number of cars at the lowest possible cost and in the shortest amount of time.

In the first rudimentary assembly line, an empty chassis was pulled across the factory floor using a rope and winch, with 140 workers positioned at various points along the 45-metre (147-foot) line to install the car's 3,000 different components. Each worker was trained to perform one particular task well, such as installing a radiator or a light, before the vehicle was moved on to the next station to have the next fitting attached.

The simplicity of the production line allowed unskilled employees to be hired, dramatically cutting the cost of employing solely skilled workers who would demand a much higher wage. This meant that Ford was able to increase the wages he paid his staff, which rose from $2.34 to $5 a day, a rise of more than double and one that made a hugely positive social impact.

The assembly line changed the face of the automobile industry and was continually refined to improve efficiency as much as possible. The Model T was the first vehicle to be produced with this method and the car's price soon fell from $850 to less than $300. Ford's template fast became the standard and, for the first time, a comfortable and reliable car was now widely available and affordable to the average American, cementing the Model T's intended reputation as a 'car for the masses'. Car ownership boomed and the age of the automobile began.

FORD'S ASSEMBLY LINE

The production process and components that created the famous Model T

COMPONENT DELIVERY
Parts were delivered to workers' stations by chutes and feeder lines.

DASHBOARD, POWER SYSTEM AND STEERING INSTALLATION
Contrary to other US vehicles at the time, the Ford Model T featured the steering wheel on the left-hand side, which became the norm.

RAILS
The chassis was moved along the production line on rails before the wheels were added.

SUSPENSION AND AXLE INSTALLATION
The Model T featured two leaf springs, one across each axle.

ENGINE AND FUEL TANK INSTALLATION
The single-block engine design became an industry standard.

An estimated 18.5 million Model Ts were sold worldwide

Ford declared that he would "build a motor car for the great multitude"

THE EVOLUTION OF SUCCESS

The Ford Motor Company's assembly lines continued to improve

1954

By 1954, the models being manufactured in the Dearborn Assembly Plant, Michigan, were available in a multitude of colours.

1975

Ford workers at the Dearborn plant could later build and inspect their vehicles from beside the production line or from the pits below the rail.

2004

Seen here at the Flat Rock Assembly Plant, mechanisation of the assembly line led to an even more efficient production process.

A MOTOR FOR THE MASSES

The simple mechanics that helped a nation to get behind the wheel

FAST COMMUTE
The Model T could reach top speeds 65-70 kilometres (40-43 miles) per hour.

LIGHT AND STRONG
The chassis was made of a vanadium-steel alloy, creating a light yet sturdy frame.

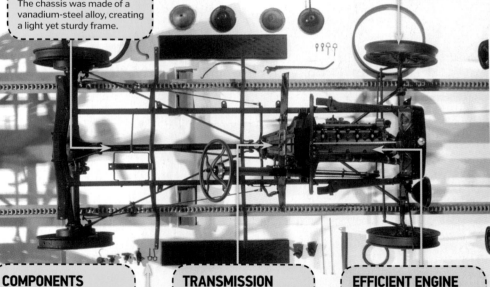

COMPONENTS
The parts fitted on the main assembly line were produced elsewhere in the factory.

TRANSMISSION
The vehicle's movement was controlled by two forward gears and one reverse gear.

EFFICIENT ENGINE
The four-cylinder engine was neatly cast in a single block.

> "FORD'S GOAL WAS TO PRODUCE THE HIGHEST NUMBER OF CARS AT THE LOWEST POSSIBLE COST"

BONNET INSTALLATION

PAINTING THE BODY
For many years the Model T was only offered in one colour. Ford remarked, "Any customer can have any colour he wants so long as it's black."

UPHOLSTERING AND VARNISHING
The wooden parts of the body were varnished and the leather upholstery added.

BODY AND CHASSIS FIXED TOGETHER

FINISHING TOUCHES
The last details were added before supervisors checked the car and engine tests were performed.

WORKERS
Workers at their stations performed the same task on each car, meaning unskilled or low-skilled labourers could be employed.

WHEELS AND RADIATOR INSTALLATION

FENDER INSTALLATION
To complete the chassis, the fenders were added and the radiator and petrol tank were filled.

BODYWORK CHAIN
The body of the car was put together on a second floor. The completed section would be lowered onto the chassis via a ramp, arches and ropes.

Image Sources • Alamy & Wallycacsabre

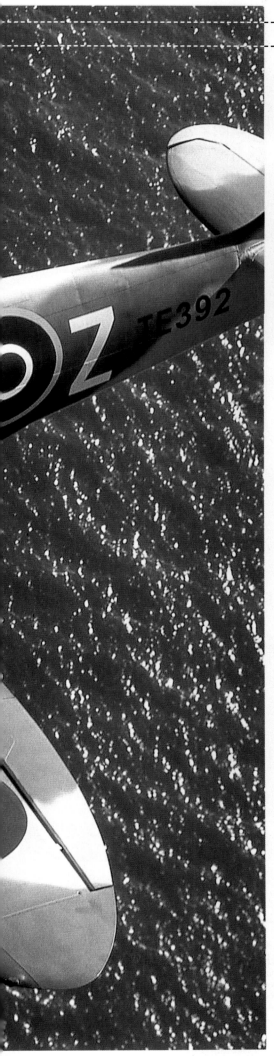

EVOLUTION OF THE RAF ◎

ON 1 APRIL 2018, THE WORLD'S FIRST INDEPENDENT AIR FORCE CELEBRATED 100 YEARS SINCE ITS FORMATION

Words by **Tim Williamson**

For over a century, the Royal Air Force has played a key role in all the major conflicts of the world, from the heroic pilots of the Battle of Britain to the fast-jet strikes of the first Gulf War. The service is almost as old as flight itself, and during its history it has remained on the cusp of the latest aviation technology, adapting to the huge shifts in tactics along the way and pushing the limits of human possibilities in the sky.

WWI ORIGINS

When the RAF was officially founded in 1918, it reformed and simplified the existing chaotic system, uniting the separate branches of the Royal Flying Corps (controlled by the Army) and the Royal Naval Air Service (controlled by the Navy). Because these two services were entirely separate entities, they had struggled to coordinate and cooperate with regards to the design and production of aircraft, or even an effective strategy for home defence.

In 1917, Jan Smuts, a member of the British War Cabinet, proposed the radical change in the organisation and command of Britain's air fleet, creating an entirely new branch of the military that would operate with its own independent hierarchy. The commissioning of aircraft models would be drawn from a single budget, meaning greater consistency and effectiveness of the designs. This new service would also bypass the rivalry between officials in the Navy and the Army, who often competed for priority over resources.

Despite this sweeping re-organisation, for the pilots on the frontline, the birth of the RAF had very little immediate effect. By 1918, airmen on both sides of no man's land had developed highly effective methods for reconnaissance as well as fighter interception. The war's vicious aerial dogfights had evolved from clumsy encounters in 1914 to fast-paced, even acrobatic dances of death. Aerial photography was already being used to great effect in reconnaissance patrols and directing artillery fire, and pilots were also regularly co-ordinating with ground forces in devastating combined arms offensives.

Just over two weeks after the formation of the RAF, the most famous and successful pilot ace of the war was finally shot down. Manfred von Richthofen, the 'Red Baron', was killed while pursuing Lieutenant Wilfrid May of 209 Squadron. Although the fatal shot was thought to have come from ground fire, the squadron nonetheless adopted a falling red eagle as its crest in honour of their vanquished foe.

The RAF's newly acquired F-35 Lightning stealth fighters were a highlights of the 2018 flypast celebrations

Image Sources • UK MOD © Crown Copyright 2018, Cpl Tim Laurence

For the last seven months of World War I, the air force would be integral to the final few campaigns on the Western Front. At the time of the Armistice in November 1918 it was one of the foremost air powers in the world, with over 293,500 personnel of all ranks and some 22,000 planes to its name.

THE FINEST HOUR OF 'THE FEW'

The inter-war years (1919-39) saw the RAF greatly reduced in strength – by 1922 it held only around 40 aircraft in service. Nonetheless, new technology and tactics continued to develop as Britain exerted its control across its empire. The first independent RAF campaign took place in 1925 in Waziristan, Pakistan. Significantly, this was also the first independent bombing campaign of the air force, foreshadowing a brutal new strategy.

In 1936 the RAF reorganised into separate Commands – Fighter, Bomber, Coastal and Training – in order to more effectively coordinate the vastly different operational requirements, such as defensive interception and offensive bombing missions. This structure would prove crucial in the coming conflict.

In another vital development that same year, the Spitfire made its debut flight from Eastleigh Aerodrome, Hampshire, displaying its incredible speed and agility in the air. Before long it would be put to the test in real combat.

Although war with Nazi Germany began in September 1939, it would be several months before the RAF could make its first significant impact. During the evacuation of over 300,000 French and British soldiers from Dunkirk in May and June 1940, Fighter Command provided vital air cover. Although outnumbered, RAF squadrons prevented the Luftwaffe from gaining air superiority over Dunkirk, which would have been catastrophic for the stranded armies. Praising this effort, Winston Churchill later asked, "May it not also be that the cause of civilisation itself will be defended by the skill and devotion of a few thousand airmen?"

Weeks later, the Luftwaffe began its daylight raids – the Battle of Britain had begun. Hurricanes and Spitfires formed the backbone of Fighter Command's squadrons, engaging formations of German bombers and their fighter escorts. On 13 August the Luftwaffe began targeting airfields with the aim of destroying the RAF's ability to fight. However, the vital work of a vast support network, and the early warning of the Radar system, meant Fighter Command's planes were kept in the air. Crucially, they could afford to remain in combat for much longer than their opponents, who had to reserve fuel for the return across the English Channel.

Also instrumental in the RAF's victory were the contributions of the many airmen from across the British Empire – as well as other Allied nations – who flew in Fighter Command squadrons. One of the most successful units during the Battle of Britain was 303 Squadron, a majority of whose pilots were Polish, forced into exile by the occupation of their country in 1939. The top-scoring fighter ace of 303 was a Czech national named Josef František, who shot down 17 planes. Thanks to Fighter Command's pilots, referred to by Churchill as 'the few' in his famous speech, by late September the Luftwaffe had abandoned its daylight raids. It instead focused on night-time sorties, beginning the Blitz of Britain's cities and industrial centres.

THE WOMEN'S AUXILIARY AIR FORCE

The Women's RAF was originally formed at the same time as the RAF in 1918, but it was discontinued in 1920 as the requirements of war ceased. However, with conflict looming once again in 1939, the Women's Auxiliary Air Force (WAAF) was formed to fill crucial roles to keep the air force flying. As well as serving as radar technicians, wireless operators, engineers and in other support roles, women also became pilots in the Air Transport Auxiliary, ferrying personnel, resources and planes across the country.

During the Battle of Britain, six WAAF personnel received the Military Medal for bravery. After the British Government enacted the conscription of women in 1941, the WAAF grew to a high of 182,000 by 1943.

BELOW WAAF personnel undergo inspection at a Fighter Command base

Image Sources • Getty

THE LIFE OF BRITAIN'S RAF

1 APRIL 1918
The Royal Air Force is officially formed, making it the world's first dedicated air force, independent of the Navy and Army.

1 APRIL 1918
The Women's Royal Naval Service and Women's Army Auxiliary Corps are merged to form the Women's Royal Air Force.

19-20 MAY 1918
84 RAF aircraft successfully fight off a German bombing raid over Britain, shooting down seven enemy airships.

14-15 JUNE 1919
RAF pilots John Alcock and Arthur Whitten Brown successfully complete the first non-stop flight across the Atlantic.

1 JANUARY 1920
An apprenticeship scheme is launched to train young technicians, engineers and a range of other RAF support roles.

RAF UNIFORMS

AIR CREW GEAR HAS TRANSFORMED FROM RUDIMENTARY TO HIGH-TECH IN UNDER A CENTURY

OXYGEN MASK
To avoid the effects of altitude sickness, aircrews each wore a mask attached to their helmet, which supplied a steady flow of oxygen.

HELMET DISPLAY
Modern helmets can display targeting and other information direct onto the pilot's visor and can be fitted with mounted displays for thermal imaging or night vision.

WARM COAT
With no enclosed cockpit, pilots had to wear thick wool- or fur-lined coats to keep warm at high altitudes.

HEADGEAR
Motoring gear was largely adopted for pilots' use. Although not much use against high-speed crashes, these helmets were handy in a bumpy landing.

THICK BOOTS
At altitudes of over 4,500 metres (14,763 feet), temperatures could drop to -30°C. Thick leather fur-lined stockings were worn to keep out the cold.

THERMAL SUIT
During WWII, bomber crews wore specially designed electrically heated suits to cope with the long periods of high-altitude flying.

RESPIRATOR
Modern respirators provide protection from biological and chemical weapons by pressurising a hood worn beneath the helmet and sealed at the neckline.

FLAME-RESISTANT
The suit was made from flame-resistant material and was also designed to be buoyant in case of a bail out over water.

ANTI-G
Modern flight suits are specially designed to counter the effects of G-force pressure at high speeds by normalising blood flow and breathing conditions.

THE MANY SUPPORTING THE FEW

ROLE 1 GROUND CREW

Each fighter plane was assigned its own ground crew team to re-fuel, repair and re-arm the aircraft between sorties. Crews would work tirelessly to repair aircraft and get them back into the battle.

ROLE 2 RADAR OPERATORS

Dozens of manned stations positioned around the coastline made up Britain's Chain Home Radar network. This acted as an early warning system to detect and report incoming enemy aircraft.

ROLE 3 FACTORY WORKERS

With thousands of men called up to serve, millions of women were called upon to power Britain's war industry. Factory assembly lines worked around the clock to produce planes, tanks, shells, artillery, weaponry and other military materiel.

ROLE 4 ANTI-AIRCRAFT

Over 1,790 light and medium anti-aircraft guns were on hand to engage enemy aircraft. Over 4,000 searchlights and 1,400 barrage balloons were also deployed to defend major cities.

Illustrations • The Art Agency/ Hemesh

9 MARCH – 1 MAY 1925
The first independent RAF operation is carried out in the form of bombing raids over Waziristan, Pakistan.

29 OCTOBER 1925
The Observer Corps is formed, tasked with detecting, identifying and reporting all aircraft movements over Britain from the ground.

5 MARCH 1936
The Supermarine Spitfire makes its first successful flight.

14 JULY 1936
RAF Bomber, Fighter and Coastal Command are formed, separating the main branches of the air force.

28 JUNE 1939
The Women's Auxiliary Air Force is formed.

10 JULY 1940
The Battle of Britain begins, with the Luftwaffe attempting to destroy the RAF's capability to defend Britain.

UNLEASHING THE WHIRLWIND

In 1942, Sir Arthur 'Bomber' Harris stated that Nazi Germany would "reap the whirlwind" in response to its devastating bombing campaigns. Between 1939 and 1945, Bomber Command carried out over 360,000 missions across Europe, targeting military installations, factories, infrastructure and eventually cities. They aimed to disrupt and destroy Germany's war industry, as well as displace and demoralise its civilians.

Up to 1,000 bombers would take part in each of these raids in order to overwhelm air defences and enemy fighters. Waves of aircraft, most often Lancaster bombers, would be led by one or two smaller pathfinder planes, which would mark the target at which the rest could aim. Throughout the war Bomber Command developed newer, deadlier payloads to deal with different targets. Industrial targets were showered with a combination of incendiary and 2,000-kilogram (4,409-pound) explosives, while reinforced submarine pens were hit with ten-ton bombs.

Several German cities suffered immeasurable damage in the whirlwind of Bomber Command's raids. Estimates of civilians killed during the campaign range from 300,000 to 1 million, and many more were made homeless. Cologne, Hamburg, Dresden and other major cities suffered some of the worst destruction in the European theatre of World War II. Witnesses recalled flaming vortexes whipping through the streets as firebombs turned neighbourhoods into infernos. However, bomber crews did not escape unscathed, with over 55,000 killed, equating to a 44 per cent casualty rate for Bomber Command.

THE JET AGE

With the start of the Cold War, Britain and its allies continued to develop and adapt to the new era of warfare dominated by the threat of nuclear arsenals. Although Nazi Germany had already deployed the world's first jet fighter during World War II, the RAF was not far behind with the Gloster Meteor, which took to the sky in the summer of 1944.

By the 1950s the air fleet had undergone its latest radical change, as the reliable old Spitfires and Hurricanes were phased out in favour of the high-speed strike fighter jets, such as the de Havilland Vampire, de Havilland Venom and Hawker Hunter. With top speeds of over 1,100 kilometres (683 miles) per hour, they were designed for much faster combat scenarios.

Bomber Command was also equipped with jet power, and its new bombers were capable of altitudes of over 16,000 metres (52,493 feet). It was also tasked with operating Britain's nuclear strike capability, and the new 'V-force' bombers (the Vulcan, Victor and Valiant) were kept in a state of constant readiness.

Although a nuclear strike was thankfully never required, during the Falklands War the Vulcan did take part in one of the longest-range

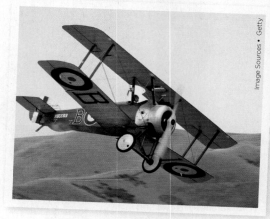

The Sopwith Camel was the RAF's WWI-era bi-plane. It was used to shoot down Zeppelin airships in 1918

RAF VS LUFTWAFFE

Both sides were equipped with pioneering aircraft

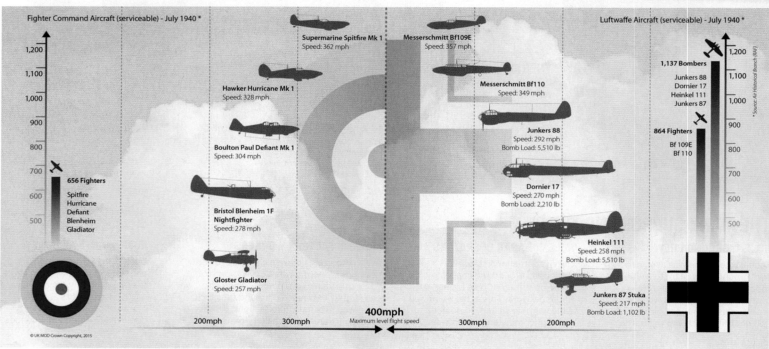

Fighter Command Aircraft (serviceable) - July 1940 *

Supermarine Spitfire Mk 1
Speed: 362 mph

Hawker Hurricane Mk 1
Speed: 328 mph

Boulton Paul Defiant Mk 1
Speed: 304 mph

656 Fighters
Spitfire
Hurricane
Defiant
Blenheim
Gladiator

Bristol Blenheim 1F Nightfighter
Speed: 278 mph

Gloster Gladiator
Speed: 257 mph

Messerschmitt Bf109E
Speed: 357 mph

Messerschmitt Bf110
Speed: 349 mph

Junkers 88
Speed: 292 mph
Bomb Load: 5,510 lb

Dornier 17
Speed: 270 mph
Bomb Load: 2,210 lb

Heinkel 111
Speed: 258 mph
Bomb Load: 5,510 lb

Junkers 87 Stuka
Speed: 217 mph
Bomb Load: 1,102 lb

Luftwaffe Aircraft (serviceable) - July 1940 *

1,137 Bombers
Junkers 88
Dornier 17
Heinkel 111
Junkers 87

864 Fighters
Bf 109E
Bf 110

200mph   300mph   **400mph** Maximum level flight speed   300mph   200mph

© UK MOD Crown Copyright, 2015

*Source: Air Historical Branch (RAF)

15 SEPTEMBER 1940
Fighter Command successfully repels the largest German raid over Britain, bringing down 176 enemy aircraft.

5 MARCH 1943
Britain's first operational jet aircraft, the Gloster Meteor, makes its first flight.

16-17 MAY 1943
Lancaster bombers from 617 Squadron successfully destroy two dams in the Rhine Valley using specially invented bouncing bombs.

30-31 MARCH 1944
Bomber Command suffers its worst losses in a single night, losing 95 aircraft during a raid on Nuremberg.

31 OCTOBER 1945
The Sikorsky R-4 helicopter, the world's first mass-produced helicopter, is air tested at RAF Andover.

1964
The Red Arrows, the Royal Air Force Aerobatic Team, is established.

FAMOUS RAF PILOTS

Leonard Cheshire
Leader of 617 Squadron, the unit that took part in the famous Dambusters raid, Cheshire became the most decorated Bomber Command pilot when he received the Victoria Cross in 1944.

Image • RAF Photographer, Stannus

Adolph 'Sailor' Malan
Born in South Africa, Malan joined the RAF in 1935 and commanded 74 Squadron during the Battle of Britain. He achieved 27 confirmed kills in the battle, and he later created his own 'Ten Rules for Air Fighting'.

Image • RAF Photographer, Trevnor

William 'Billy' Bishop
After joining the Royal Flying Corps in 1915, Bishop achieved 72 victories during WWI and also received the Victoria Cross. He later became an air marshal with the Royal Canadian Air Force during WWII. Victoria Cross in 1944.

Image • Internet Archive Book Images

Mary Ellis
After earning her pilot's licence in 1939, Ellis joined the Air Transport Auxiliary and soon became one of the first female Spitfire pilots. Although she was not strictly in the RAF itself, she delivered over 1,000 planes during the war.

Image • Getty

Witold Urbanowicz
Already a battle-hardened pilot, Urbanowicz commanded the majority-Polish 303 Squadron in 1940. He achieved a total of 15 victories during the battle and was awarded the Distinguished Flying Cross.

Image • Alamy

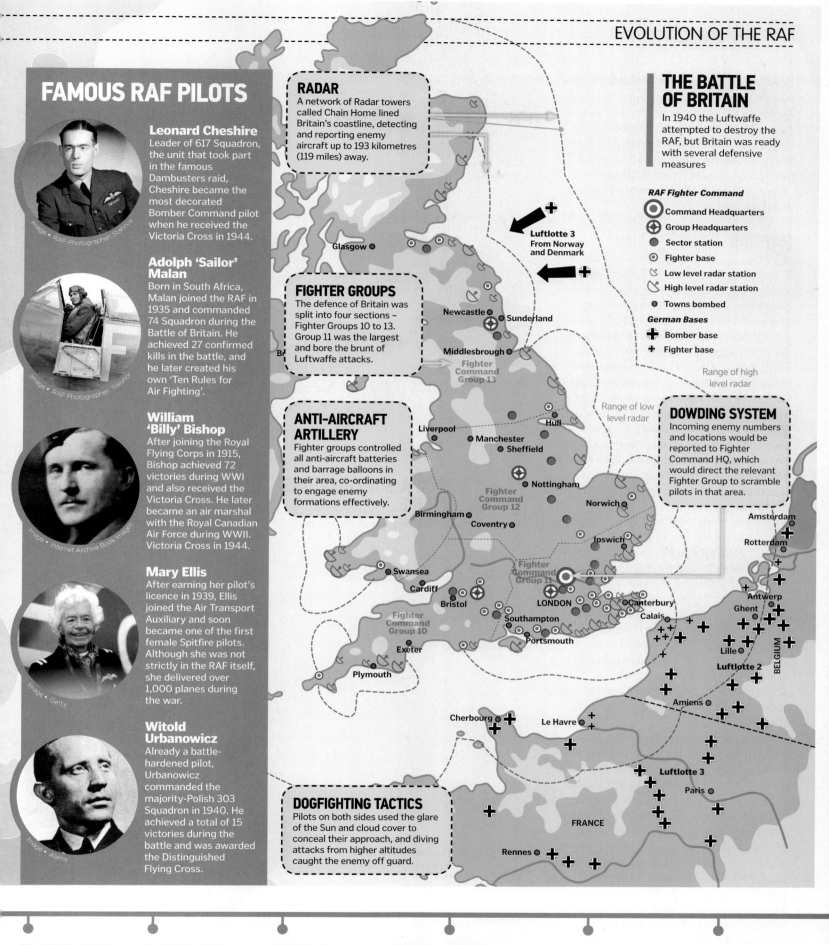

RADAR
A network of Radar towers called Chain Home lined Britain's coastline, detecting and reporting enemy aircraft up to 193 kilometres (119 miles) away.

FIGHTER GROUPS
The defence of Britain was split into four sections – Fighter Groups 10 to 13. Group 11 was the largest and bore the brunt of Luftwaffe attacks.

ANTI-AIRCRAFT ARTILLERY
Fighter groups controlled all anti-aircraft batteries and barrage balloons in their area, co-ordinating to engage enemy formations effectively.

DOGFIGHTING TACTICS
Pilots on both sides used the glare of the Sun and cloud cover to conceal their approach, and diving attacks from higher altitudes caught the enemy off guard.

THE BATTLE OF BRITAIN
In 1940 the Luftwaffe attempted to destroy the RAF, but Britain was ready with several defensive measures

RAF Fighter Command
- Command Headquarters
- Group Headquarters
- Sector station
- Fighter base
- Low level radar station
- High level radar station
- Towns bombed

German Bases
- Bomber base
- Fighter base

DOWDING SYSTEM
Incoming enemy numbers and locations would be reported to Fighter Command HQ, which would direct the relevant Fighter Group to scramble pilots in that area.

Range of high level radar

Range of low level radar

Luftlotte 3 From Norway and Denmark

Glasgow

Newcastle Sunderland

Middlesbrough

Fighter Command Group 13

Liverpool Hull

Manchester
Sheffield

Fighter Command Group 12

Nottingham

Norwich

Birmingham
Coventry

Ipswich

Swansea

Cardiff

Fighter Command Group 11

Bristol

LONDON Canterbury

Fighter Command Group 10

Southampton Calais

Portsmouth

Exeter

Plymouth

Amsterdam

Rotterdam

Antwerp
Ghent

Lille

Luftlotte 2

BELGIUM

Cherbourg Le Havre

Amiens

Luftlotte 3

Paris

FRANCE

Rennes

30 APRIL 1968
RAF Bomber and Fighter Command merge to form Strike Command.

1 APRIL 1969
The world's first vertical take-off and landing aircraft, the Harrier, enters RAF service.

30 APRIL – 1 MAY 1982
Vulcan jets attack targets on the Falkland Islands, conducting at the time the longest-range bombing operation in history.

1990
RAF aircraft take part in Operation Granby – British operations during the 1990–91 Gulf War.

2007
The first RAF operations using Reaper MQ-9A drones are conducted in Afghanistan.

2018
RAF 617 Squadron is re-formed, equipped with the F-35B Lightning.

missions in RAF history. Operation Black Buck was a series of bombing runs launched from Ascension Island in the central Atlantic Ocean, covering 6,100 kilometres (3,790 miles) to the target: Port Stanley airfield on the Falklands. This was followed up with attacks from nine Sea Harriers, another iconic British aircraft of the era that was capable of vertical take-off and landing.

RAF 100

Since the turn of the century, the RAF has kept in step with the advances in unmanned aircraft systems, and it joined the MQ-9A Reaper drone programme in 2004. Although the concept of unmanned air vehicles (UAVs) is nothing new, the capabilities of this latest leap in technology marks the start of a new era for the world's air forces. Reaper drones can conduct precise intelligence gathering and offensive missions, identifying and targeting enemy positions, all while under the control of a ground crew that is often thousands of miles away. The next generation of drone systems, the Predator SkyGuardian, has already made history as the first medium-altitude long-endurance (MALE) craft to cross the Atlantic, arriving at RAF Fairford in July 2018.

For some, these unmanned systems mark the future of aerial warfare. However, for now at least the core of the air force remains its piloted strike fighters. In 2018, the legendary 617 Squadron, the Dambusters, was reformed and received its first F-35 Lightning jet fighters. These aircraft reflect the multi-role demands of the modern era, with stealth design features, electronic warfare capability and advanced avionics enabling the F-35 to take on nearly any mission. The Fleet Air Arm will also be deploying the short take-off and landing variant of the F-35 for use with the Queen Elizabeth class aircraft carriers.

During the centenary year of the RAF celebrations commemorating the milestone were held throughout Britain. This included a country-wide tour of some of the force's most famous machines. On 10 July over 100 aircraft took part in a spectacular flypast over London. This included modern aircraft such as the Eurofighter and F-35, following on the tails of historic icons such as the Spitfire and Lancaster bomber (all part of the Battle of Britain Memorial Flight). The Red Arrows also took part, as well as the Chinook and a range of utility helicopters. This one display represented nearly 100 years of military history, demonstrating the RAF's greatest accomplishments and embodying its motto, 'Per ardua ad astra': Through adversity to the stars.

Illustration • Getty

The remotely controlled Reaper drone came into RAF service in 2004

Image Sources • Sgt Corinne Buxton RAF/MOD

INSIDE A SUPERMARINE SPITFIRE

The RAF's iconic aircraft was one of the greatest fighter planes of WWII

COCKPIT
The airframe was recognisable for its aerodynamic, domed canopy, although without a pressurised cockpit pilots could not achieve higher altitudes.

The Eurofighter Typhoon entered RAF service in 2006 and remains active in several squadrons

Image Sources • Getty

Hurricane pilots rush to their machines after being scrambled for take-off, August 1939

Members of 106 Squadron, Bomber Command, pose in front of a Lancaster Bomber, March 1943

Image Sources • Getty

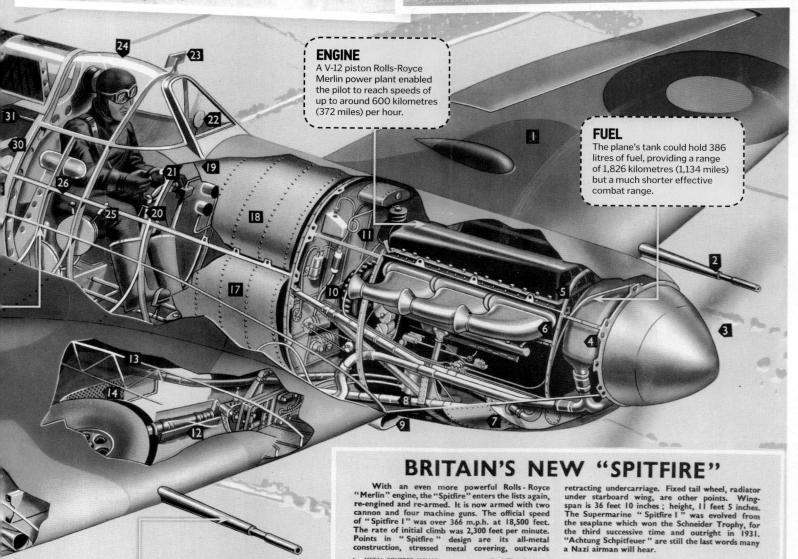

ENGINE
A V-12 piston Rolls-Royce Merlin power plant enabled the pilot to reach speeds of up to around 600 kilometres (372 miles) per hour.

FUEL
The plane's tank could hold 386 litres of fuel, providing a range of 1,826 kilometres (1,134 miles) but a much shorter effective combat range.

ARMAMENT
Mounted on the wings were two Hispano 20mm cannons and four Browning 7.7mm machine guns.

BRITAIN'S NEW "SPITFIRE"

With an even more powerful Rolls-Royce "Merlin" engine, the "Spitfire" enters the lists again, re-engined and re-armed. It is now armed with two cannon and four machine guns. The official speed of "Spitfire I" was over 366 m.p.h. at 18,500 feet. The rate of initial climb was 2,300 feet per minute. Points in "Spitfire" design are its all-metal construction, stressed metal covering, outwards retracting undercarriage. Fixed tail wheel, radiator under starboard wing, are other points. Wing-span is 36 feet 10 inches; height, 11 feet 5 inches. The Supermarine "Spitfire I" was evolved from the seaplane which won the Schneider Trophy, for the third successive time and outright in 1931. "Achtung Schpitfeuer" are still the last words many a Nazi airman will hear.

1	METAL-COVERED WINGS	13	METAL RIBS	24	SLIDING HOOD
2	CANNON	14	RADIATOR	25	UNDERCARRIAGE CONTROL HANDLE
3	THREE-BLADED CONSTANT-SPEED AIR SCREW	15	MACHINE GUNS	26	LONGERON
		16	AILERON	27	BATTERY BOX
4	TANK	17	LOWER FUEL TANK	28	PARACHUTE FLARE
5	ROLLS-ROYCE "MERLIN" ENGINE	18	UPPER FUEL TANK	29	METAL RIBS
6	EXHAUSTS	19	INSTRUMENT PANEL	30	DITTY BOX
7	OIL TANK	20	CONTROL LEVER	31	STRINGER
8	ENGINE BEARERS	21	FIRING TRIGGER	32	RADIO
9	CARBURETTOR AIR INTAKE	22	GUN SIGHT	33	AERIAL
10	SUPERCHARGER	23	MIRROR	34	FIN
11	FIREPROOF BULKHEAD			35	RUDDER
12	RETRACTED UNDERCARRIAGE (STARBOARD)		LENGTH 29 ft. 11 in.	36	ELEVATORS
			SPAN OF PLANES 36 ft. 10 in.	37	TAIL WHEEL

Total Fuel Load — 85 Gallons

100 YEARS OF WARFARE TANKS

THE EVOLUTION OF ARMOURED BATTLE, FROM WWI TO MODERN MECHANISED MARVELS

Ancient Greek hoplites joined their shields and advanced in unison. Hannibal's Carthaginians mounted war elephants. The visionary Leonardo da Vinci rendered an image of an armoured fighting vehicle in 1487. While the concept of the tank – an armoured unit that could dominate the battlefield – has existed for almost as long as mankind has waged war, it became workable and developed to devastating capability 100 years ago.

Since the creaky bathtubs of World War I, the tank has existed to provide an operational edge during combat. Its varied roles range from the hammer blow of the mailed fist to break through enemy lines, to the rapid exploitation of the breach and the destruction of other vehicles and fortifications, as well as reconnaissance and fire support as mobile artillery.

To successfully complete the assigned mission, tanks require three key design elements: firepower, mobility and protection. Concentrated firepower punches a hole through enemy lines, while being able to tackle any type of terrain at speed enables them to travel over enemy trenches, and heavy armour shields the crew that supplies the expertise, efficiency and courage to go in harm's way.

When the tank entered combat for the first time, hopes were high that the horrific stalemate of trench warfare would be broken. While the tank matured as an armament system, it became a weapon of dominance and decision. Today, it is perceived both as a potential war winner and a costly machine that may be past its prime. Regardless, the technological advancements and its impact on warfare are nothing short of astonishing.

Without question, the mere existence of the tank continues to influence any decision to wage war and any effective defence against an attacker on land. The tank, therefore, remains a prime shaper of military strategy and will continue to be into the foreseeable future.

TANKS THROUGH HISTORY
Over decades of warfare, technology has shaped tanks into weapons of awesome power

Mark V (Male)
Country of origin: United Kingdom
First produced: 1917
Still in service? No

Char B1 bis
Country of origin: France
First produced: 1937
Still in service? No

Centurion
Country of origin: United Kingdom
First produced: 1945
Still in service?: No

M60
Country of origin: United States
First produced: 1959
Still in service? Yes

PT-76
Country of origin: Soviet Union
First produced: 1950
Still in service? Yes

T-54
Country of origin: Soviet Union
First produced: 1948
Still in service? Yes

T-72
Country of origin: Soviet Union
First produced: 1971
Still in service? Yes

Leopard 2
Country of origin: Germany
First produced: 1979
Still in service? Yes

M1A1 Abrams
Country of origin: United States
First produced: 1979
Still in service? Yes

Challenger 2
Country of origin: United Kingdom
First produced: 1993
Still in service? Yes

Arjun
Country of origin: India
First produced: 2004
Still in service? Yes

K2 Black Panther
Country of origin: South Korea
First produced: 2013
Still in service? Yes

T-90
Country of origin: Russia
First produced: 1993
Still in service? Yes

Illustrations • Nicholas Forder

Challenger 2 is equipped with a highly accurate fire control system

Illustrations • Cpl Si Longworth RLC / MOD

Illustrations • U.S. Navy photo by Photographer's Mate 1st Class Michael Larson

The T-72 tank has been exported to over 30 countries

TANKS PAST AND PRESENT

HOW THE DEMANDS OF THE MODERN BATTLEFIELD HAVE SHAPED DESIGNS

Prior to World War I, research and development yielded some practical benefits in tank design. Caterpillar treads, already in use with heavy tractors, proved superior to wheels, and power to weight ratios had a significant impact on mobility and performance.

Experimentation with every aspect of the tank's development led to the introduction of basic internal power plants, and sheets of steel were riveted together to form armoured boxes on top of a tractor or car chassis. Visibility and steering were crudely accomplished with hazardous viewing ports and a series of tillers respectively. Machine guns and cannon originally meant for use with infantry and artillery units were also adapted.

Although they were terrifying to the common foot soldier that encountered them, the earliest tanks were heavy and unwieldy contraptions that were prone to mechanical failures. The engines were simply inadequate for propelling the tremendous weight of the vehicle forward, and the exhaust fumes from straining engines sometimes even sickened the crews so seriously that they could not function.

The second generation of armoured vehicles reflected the experience of the Great War, and numerous innovations of the interwar years were put to use during World War II. The purpose-built tank chassis was refined, diesel and gasoline engines became more powerful and some were borrowed from the aircraft industry. The rotating turret-mounted machine guns and cannons were introduced and armour protection improved, while communication between tanks was vastly enhanced with reliable radios that replaced hand signals and directional flags.

During the second half of the 20th century and beyond, evolving technology has transformed the tank into a modern marvel of mechanised warfare. GPS fosters unprecedented coordination of units, while sophisticated infrared target acquisition and stabilisation equipment allow tanks to track multiple targets simultaneously and accurately fire weapons on the move. They also feature state-of-the-art turbine engines combined with composite armour – lighter and many times stronger than steel – for unprecedented speed and security.

Image Source • John Warwick Broo

Image Source • Getty

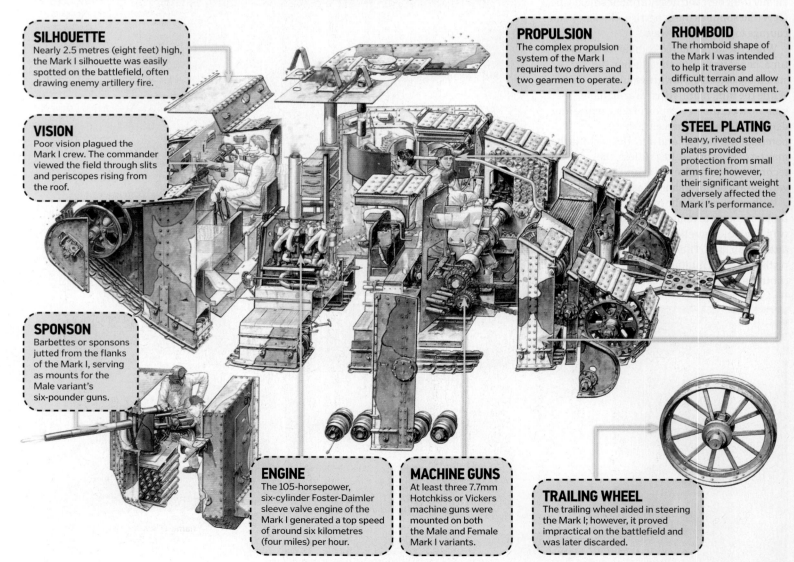

SILHOUETTE
Nearly 2.5 metres (eight feet) high, the Mark I silhouette was easily spotted on the battlefield, often drawing enemy artillery fire.

VISION
Poor vision plagued the Mark I crew. The commander viewed the field through slits and periscopes rising from the roof.

SPONSON
Barbettes or sponsons jutted from the flanks of the Mark I, serving as mounts for the Male variant's six-pounder guns.

PROPULSION
The complex propulsion system of the Mark I required two drivers and two gearmen to operate.

RHOMBOID
The rhomboid shape of the Mark I was intended to help it traverse difficult terrain and allow smooth track movement.

STEEL PLATING
Heavy, riveted steel plates provided protection from small arms fire; however, their significant weight adversely affected the Mark I's performance.

ENGINE
The 105-horsepower, six-cylinder Foster-Daimler sleeve valve engine of the Mark I generated a top speed of around six kilometres (four miles) per hour.

MACHINE GUNS
At least three 7.7mm Hotchkiss or Vickers machine guns were mounted on both the Male and Female Mark I variants.

TRAILING WHEEL
The trailing wheel aided in steering the Mark I; however, it proved impractical on the battlefield and was later discarded.

1916 MARK I

The first tank ended the stalemate of trench warfare

Hopes of breaking the agonising stalemate of trench warfare during World War I led to the accelerated development of the world's first operational tank, the British Mark I. The Landship Committee was established in 1915 by Winston Churchill – First Lord of the Admiralty at the time – to produce an armoured vehicle for the battlefield. The Mark I was the production model of earlier prototypes Little Willie and Mother.

The Mark I weighed just over 28 tons and was powered by a six-cylinder Foster-Daimler engine. It was produced in two variants, the Male mounting two Hotchkiss six-pounder guns and the Female mounting two Vickers machine guns, with both variants sporting an additional three light machine guns.

Eight crew shared a common compartment. The British Army placed the first order for 100 Mark I tanks in February 1916, and the tank made its combat debut during the Battle of the Somme. Although several tanks broke down or became stranded, a new era in modern warfare had begun.

Image Source • Der Weltkrieg im Bild. Verlag: Knaur, Leipzig 1920

The first tanks were designed to break through barbed wire on enemy lines

Conditions inside a Mark I were hot, noisy and dangerous for the eight-man crew

Image Source • Ernest Brooks

Image Source • National Archives at College Park

An American crew awaits orders for a light tank in Coburg, Germany in 1945

Image Source • Life Magazine photographer Mark Kauffman

M4 Sherman tanks equipped with flame-throwers were deployed by the US in the Battle of Iwo Jima in 1945

Image Source • Shane A. Cuomo, U.S. Air Force

PRESENT DAY CHALLENGER 2
The main battle tank of the British Army

Considered by many military analysts to be the finest main battle tank in the world today, the development of the British Challenger 2 occurred during a five-year period from 1986 to 1991. Although it shares a common name with its predecessor, the Challenger 1, less than five per cent of the components are compatible.

Designed as a battlefield supremacy tank, the Challenger 2 weighs just under 70 tons and is the first British tank since World War II to be designed, developed and put into production by a single principal defence contractor, the Land

Systems Division of BAE Systems. The main weapon of the Challenger 2 is the 120mm L30 CHARM (CHallenger main ARMament) rifled gun, and control of the turret and gun are maintained through solid-state electronics.

The tank is also equipped with smaller weapons, including a coaxial L94A1 7.62mm chain gun and a 7.62mm L37A2 commander's machine gun. Protected by second generation Chobham composite armour, the Challenger 2 has compiled an impressive combat record, primarily during Operation Iraqi Freedom.

TARGET ACQUISITION
The commander and gunner of the Challenger 2 utilise gyrostabilised, fully panoramic gunsights with thermal imaging and laser range finding.

Image Source • Steve Dock/MOD

The British Challenger 2 was produced from 1993 to 2002, and approximately 450 units were completed

DRIVER POSITION
One of four Challenger 2 crewmen, the driver sits at the front and uses the periscope and night vision to steer the tank.

The Japanese Type 90 tank delivers 1,500 horsepower, as much as the Bugatti Chiron, the fastest car in the world

MAIN ARMAMENT
The main weapon of the Challenger 2 is the 120mm L30 rifled cannon equipped with a thermal sleeve to prevent warping.

SUSPENSION
A hydro-gas variable spring rate suspension provides stability for the Challenger 2 in cross-country action or on the road.

TRACKS
Tension in the Challenger 2's tracks can be hydraulically adjusted from the driver's compartment, to provide excellent mobility on various terrains.

Image Source • Rikurojieitai Koudisho

"TECHNOLOGY HAS TRANSFORMED THE TANK INTO A MODERN MARVEL OF WARFARE"

SECONDARY ARMAMENT

A pair of 7.62mm machine guns mounted at the loader's hatch provide close defence for the Challenger 2.

TURRET

The aerodynamic Challenger 2 turret houses sophisticated vision, target acquisition and defensive systems, along with seating for the commander and the gunner.

Image Source • Lance Corporal [...]

The M1 Abrams has served in the Cold War, Iraq and Afghanistan and is predicted to be in use until 2050

Image Source • U.S. Air Force photo/ Master Sgt. Mitch G[...]

ENGINE

The 1,200-horsepower, 12-cylinder Perkins-Condor CV12 diesel engine of the Challenger 2 generates a top speed of 60 kilometres per hour.

In 2007, Canada borrowed 20 Leopard C2 tanks from Germany to aid their troops in Afghanistan

Image Source • Sgt. Paul L. Anstine III, U.S. Marine Corps

Despite their high-tech defences, modern tanks can still succumb to enemy fire

Illustration • Alex Pang

Image Source • Cpl Si Longworth RLC / MOD

Challenger 2 entered service with the British Army in 1998

LAYERED ARMOUR

Certain characteristics of the improved composite armour protecting the Challenger 2 remain classified.

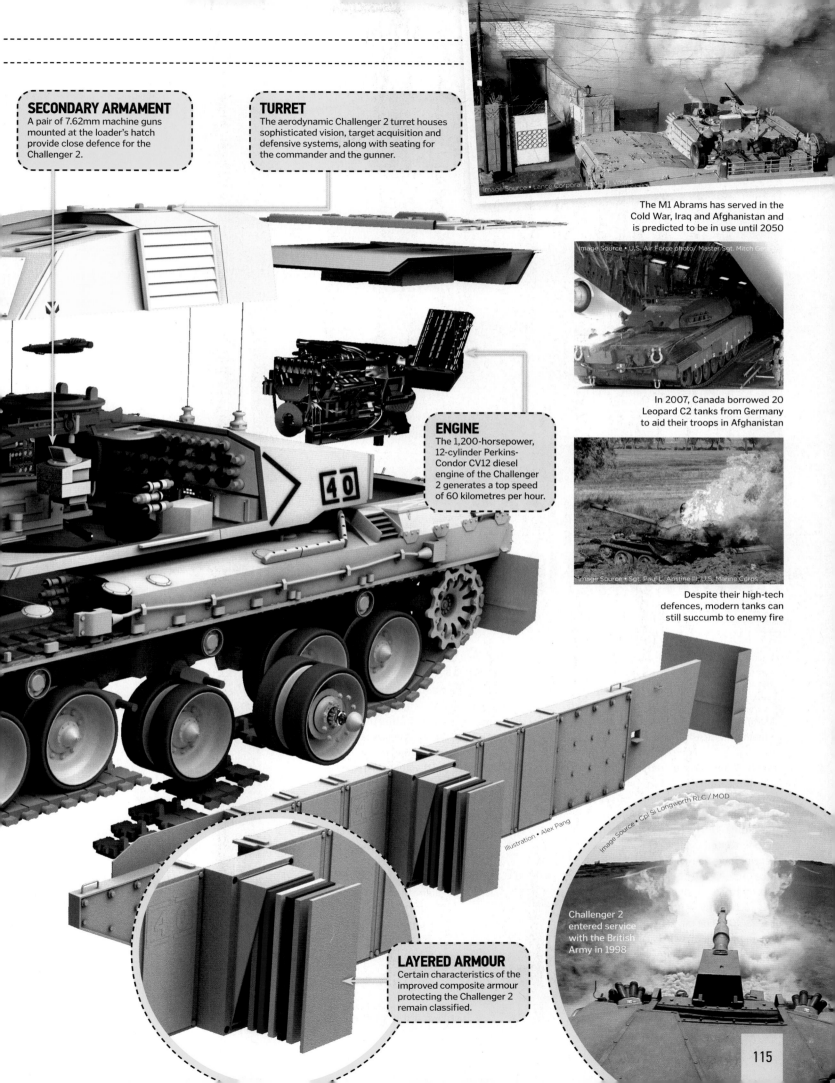

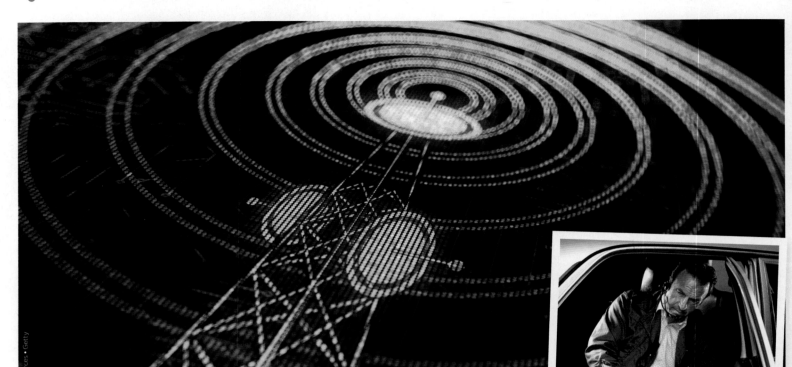

RUSSIA'S GHOST RADIO STATION

A MYSTERIOUS SHORTWAVE SIGNAL IS BROADCASTING AN EERIE BUZZ, BUT NOBODY KNOWS WHY

A short, monotonous buzz being broadcast 24 hours a day is currently being emitted from a radio station at an unknown location in Russia. The mysterious sound repeats at a rate of 25 times a minute, broken only by the occasional live Russian voice transmission. Is the signal used for military communications, perhaps just a channel marker to keep the frequency busy so it is easier to use? Or is the sound the result of something more sinister? The earliest known recording has been dated to 1982, and many theories have been proposed since then.

Its original call sign was UVB-76, but today the tower uses ZhUOZ. The buzz is broken by Russian words, but they offer no real clue as to the function of the radio or its origins. They are often common nouns, including 'virus' and 'prison'.

It sounds like a code, but the Russian military claim they have nothing to do with the mysterious signal.

Perhaps the most chilling theory is that the tone might be what is known as a 'Dead Hand' signal, a system designed to automatically retaliate with deadly nuclear strikes in response to a nuclear attack on Russia, which would be picked up by radio wave interference. This system was first devised by the Soviet Union during the Cold War era, and some experts suggest it may still be in use today.

Regardless of its origins, there must be someone behind the signal and there must be someone tuning into the live transmission who knows the real reason why the broadcast is being sent out. The question is who?

The exact source location of the signal is unknown, and it's thought to have moved on at least one occasion

A similarly strange radio signal, broadcast from Cyprus between the 1970s and 2008, is believed to have been operated by the British Secret Intelligence Service

CLUES FROM THE BUZZER

The only clues about the purpose of this tower come from the sound of the signal itself. We know that the buzz continues 24 hours a day, seven days a week, 365 days a year, and it has done so for at least three decades. During this time the sound has altered occasionally and sometimes even paused for brief periods, but it has never fully stopped.

We know that UVB-76 became more vocal after the fall of communism in Russia – which may give a hint of a political identity – and after the turn of the millennium even more communications were heard over the frequency. With the increase in global interest from radio enthusiasts, it has become evident the sound isn't recorded. Instead, it is being created manually by a tonewheel and picked up by a microphone. If you listen long enough to the broadcast you can very occasionally hear muffled conversations or sounds of things moving in the background.

Other notable events include approximately 24 hours of eerie silence on 5 June 2010, and in September 2010 the station was moved and began to use the new call sign of MDZhB. On 11 November 2010, a conversation involving 'bridge operative officer on duty' was broadcast – it is suspected that this was accidental.

All Image Sources • Getty

CASSETTE TAPES AND PLAYERS

THE RETRO DEVICE THAT MADE MUSIC PORTABLE BEFORE THE INTRODUCTION OF CD AND MP3 PLAYERS

Cassette players were initially designed for use as dictation machines, but were soon adopted as music players. These devices contained sprockets (to wind the cassette tape), a capstan (to control the speed of the tape) and, most importantly, the record and playback heads; tiny electromagnets that turned sound into magnetic patterns and vice versa.

The tape inside audio cassettes contains iron oxide, a ferromagnetic material, meaning it can be permanently magnetised. When recording audio, a microphone converts sound waves into a changing voltage, which is then boosted by an amplifier. The electrical output from the amplifier is sent to the recording head. The varying voltage causes the recording head to generate a changing magnetic field, which the tape passes through as it moves from one reel to the other. As the tape moves by the recording head, the iron oxide grains in it align in the direction of the magnetic field, producing a pattern that represents the changing sounds detected by the microphone.

Playback essentially involves the reverse of this process. As a magnetised tape passes by the playback head, its recorded pattern induces a voltage in the electromagnet, so the magnetically-aligned pattern on the tape can be 'read' and converted into a voltage. This signal is then amplified and sent to a speaker to reproduce the audio that was initially recorded.

Tape recorders also contain an erase function, which feeds an ultrasonic signal to the tape to remove any alignment patterns from past recordings. The flexibility of being able to tape over old recordings, combined with their compact size, are among the reasons why cassettes players became such popular gadgets among music lovers on the move .

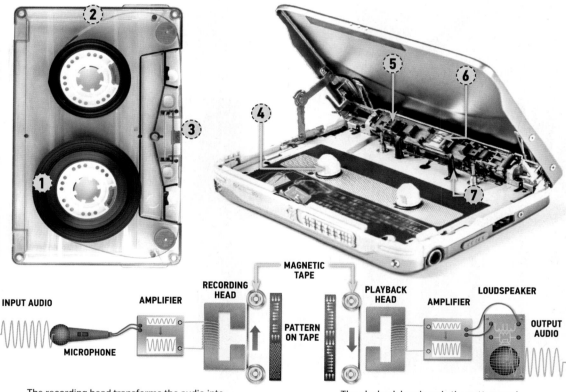

The recording head transforms the audio into a specific pattern on the magnetic tape...

...The playback head reads the pattern and translates this back into the original audio signal

INPUT AUDIO — MICROPHONE — AMPLIFIER — RECORDING HEAD — MAGNETIC TAPE — PATTERN ON TAPE — PLAYBACK HEAD — AMPLIFIER — LOUDSPEAKER — OUTPUT AUDIO

Illustrations • Alex Phoenix

1 SUPPLY REEL
The tape is fed from the supply wheel and into the take-up reel as the sound recording plays.

2 TAPE
The tape is coated in a lubricant to prevent it wearing out the other parts.

3 PRESSURE PAD
This small, spongy pad makes sure that the magnetic tape maintains good contact with the record or playback head.

4 SPROCKETS
These connect to the spools and spin to move the tape during playback, recording, fast-forward or rewind.

5 ERASE HEAD
This electromagnet is powered by a high-frequency source to remove any recordings already on the tape so the cassette can be re-used.

6 ELECTROMAGNET
The record and playback heads are two small electromagnets that can write on or read the magnetic tape respectively.

7 CAPSTAN
The capstan spins at a precise rate to control the tape speed, ensuring the music is recorded or played at the intended speed.

THE EVOLUTION OF PORTABLE MUSIC

Image • Gregory F. Maxwell

1954
The Regency TR-1 was the first transistor radio available on the consumer market and the first truly portable mass-market radio.

Image • Binarysequence

1979
The audio cassette tape went portable in 1979 with the release of the Sony Walkman, which became a global success.

Image • Morn

1984
In 1984 the first Sony Discman was released, helping increase the popularity of CDs as an audio storage medium.

Image • Evan-Amos

1992
MiniDiscs were effectively downsized CDs, but this technology eventually lost out to the MP3 players that were introduced in the late 1990s.

Image • BoH

2001
The first-generation iPod was unveiled, offering an unprecedented '1,000 songs in your pocket'.

NUCLEAR BUNKERS

DISCOVER THE SECRETS OF THESE PROTECTIVE UNDERGROUND FACILITIES
THAT COULD PRESERVE LIFE IN THE EVENT OF A NUCLEAR HOLOCAUST

U ntil recently, nuclear bunkers were considered relics of the Cold War, as indeed most of them are. But with increasing tension between North Korea and the US, perhaps these fallout shelters don't seem quite so irrelevant any more. Here we delve into the world of nuclear bunkers, with particular reference to those large facilities designed to provide military and governmental control centres in the event of conflict.

Although the threat of nuclear war tends to be associated with the period between the end of the Second World War and the breakup of the Soviet Union in 1991, nuclear bunkers can trace their heritage back to earlier conflicts. The

"PERHAPS FALLOUT SHELTERS DON'T SEEM QUITE SO IRRELEVANT ANY MORE"

phrase 'trench warfare' epitomises the First World War, but excavations in Flanders Fields also included underground bunkers that were used as command centres, shelters and stores for ammunition and food. However, it was due to the threat of bombing to the UK during the Second World War that underground defences really got a foothold. These sub-surface structures ranged from large facilities – such as Churchill's well-known Cabinet War Rooms – to the Anderson shelters that people were encouraged to bury in their own gardens to provide protection against air raids.

The design of a bunker capable of protecting its inhabitants from a conventional bomb isn't too demanding. Unless it suffers a direct hit, the protection afforded by a few metres of earth is generally adequate to prevent severe injury. As we turn our attention to a bunker capable of offering immunity from a nuclear attack, though, the requirements become a lot more stringent, as will become evident if we think about the result of a nuclear explosion.

First of all there'd be an explosive force that would be much more powerful than that caused by a conventional bomb. A nuclear blast would result in a hugely powerful shock wave, effectively a blast of wind that could exceed 1,000 kilometres (621 miles) per hour, plus the risk of falling buildings and flying debris. Simultaneously with the physical blast, an intense flash of thermal radiation would be generated. This would result in fires over a wide area and could be capable of causing instantaneous severe burns to people to a distance of ten kilometres (six miles) or more

from ground zero depending on the size of the bomb. But the immediate effect is just the beginning.

A nuclear explosion releases gamma rays, alpha and beta particles, neutrons and heavy radioactive species, and it also carries material from the ground up into the mushroom cloud, where it becomes contaminated by nuclear material. This then drops back to the surface over a period of time in a phenomenon referred to as 'fallout'. The heavier, more dangerous debris falls back down within a matter of minutes, whereas the smaller fallout particles, invisible to the naked eye, are small enough to be inhaled into a person's lungs, with the potential to cause serious injury. Because a detonation will typically occur at an altitude of several kilometres and such tiny particles could stay airborne for weeks, the result is that the region around the detonation (and perhaps up to many hundreds of kilometres) could be hazardous to human life for an extended period of time.

The implication of this is that, while nuclear bunkers certainly need to offer protection against a powerful blast, they also need to provide protection from radiation and an

The telephone exchange at the UK's Cold War Emergency Government War Headquarters in Corsham, Wiltshire

isolated living environment for several months, perhaps up to a year, until the surrounding area recovers sufficiently to permit human habitation. Nuclear bunkers, especially those used for military and government purposes, also require communication capabilities. Among other things, a bunker would require protection from an EMP, an electromagnetic pulse that would shut down any electronic equipment unless it was properly protected against such an event.

BBC radio broadcasting equipment in the Kelvedon Hatch nuclear bunker

BBC'S WARTIME BROADCASTING SYSTEM

To provide a service in the event of nuclear war, from the 1950s the BBC drew up plans for a Wartime Broadcasting Service. Around the country were 11 regional seats of government, housed in protected bunkers; the BBC had a studio in each, manned by staff from local radio stations. Overall control would have been from a bunker at the Engineering Training Department at Wood Norton in Worcestershire.

According to a BBC report following declassification of the service, the most recent

recorded announcement by Radio 4 newsreader Peter Donaldson contained the statement, "This is the Wartime Broadcasting Service. This country has been attacked with nuclear weapons. Communications have been severely disrupted, and the number of casualties and the extent of the damage are not yet known. We shall bring you further information as soon as possible. Meanwhile, stay tuned to this wavelength, stay calm and stay in your own homes. There is nothing to be gained by trying to get away."

Advice on the construction of a bunker capable of providing protection against nuclear attack was published in 1979 by America's Oak Ridge National Laboratory. Generally speaking, blast protection is achieved with adequate ground cover, perhaps by digging the shelter and then building an arched roof capable of supporting the weight of a mound of earth that covers the bunker. This cover of earth will also offer a good degree of protection against radiation risks. The advice gave particular attention to the door, which would otherwise undermine the protection. In particular, a blast door is needed to keep out blast waves, blast wind, over-pressure, blast-borne debris, burning hot dust and fallout. Some advice also suggested making tunnels as labyrinthine as possible as means of reducing the amount of radiation entering the shelter through them.

Moving beyond the immediate effect of the blast, advice was given on the provision of a living space for prolonged occupation. This meant stockpiling food that would last for months, perhaps even longer, and also providing an adequate supply of water. The air supply is also an issue, which means that an air pump and filtration system would have been required. Because of the uncertainty over the survival of power generation and mains distribution facilities, provision was required for manual operation.

While Second World War air raid shelters were intended to protect civilians, Cold War nuclear bunkers tended to be much larger facilities designed for military and government purposes. A list of over 700 disused establishments compiled by Subterranea Britannica reveals a broad range of purposes

Cheyenne Mountain's blast doors are designed to protect against a nuclear attack, among other threats

SPRING MOUNTINGS
The buildings are clear of the mountain walls, resting on 1,319 springs to absorb vibrations caused by an explosion.

INTERNAL BUILDINGS
The complex contains 15 steel buildings, most are three storeys high.

INTERNAL BUILDING

INSIDE THE CHEYENNE MOUNTAIN COMPLEX
The secrets of one of the world's best-known high-security nuclear bunkers

SVALBARD GLOBAL SEED VAULT

Way up above the Arctic Circle, on the island of Spitsbergen in the Norwegian territory of Svalbard, lies the Global Seed Vault. Built in an abandoned coal mine that burrows its way under a mountain, the facility is intended to protect the seeds of food crops not only against natural catastrophes and war, but also avoidable disasters such as a lack of funding or poor management.

Its location just 1,300 kilometres (807 miles) from the North Pole takes it well away from any likely nuclear targets, but that wasn't the main reason for picking this most remote island. The ambient temperature allows the seeds to be stored at the optimal temperature of -18 degrees Celsius (-0.4 degrees Fahrenheit) without the expense of refrigeration.

At the time of writing, the vault has 986,243 samples in storage, originating from almost every country in the world, and it aims to offer options for future generations to overcome the challenges of climate change and population growth.

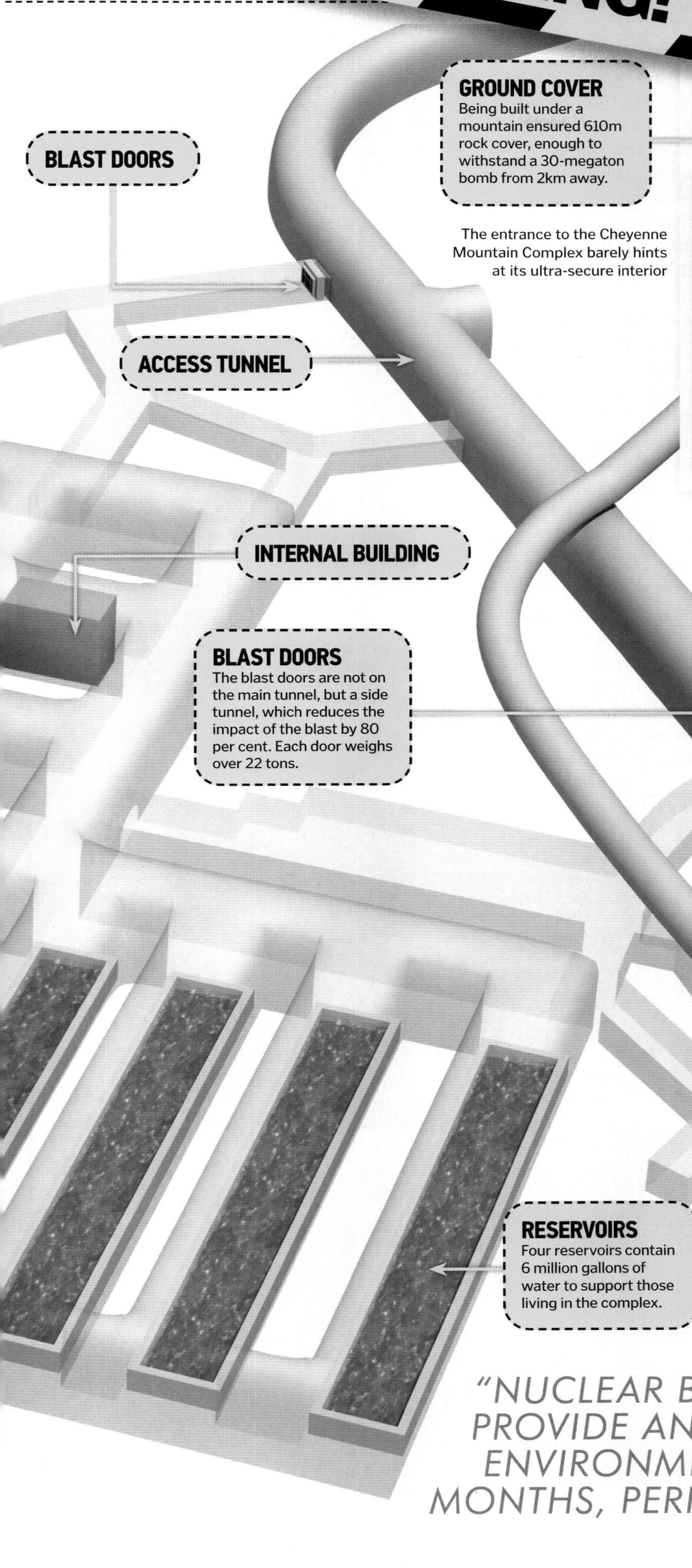

WARNING! ☠ WARNING! ☠ WA

BLAST DOORS

GROUND COVER
Being built under a mountain ensured 610m rock cover, enough to withstand a 30-megaton bomb from 2km away.

The entrance to the Cheyenne Mountain Complex barely hints at its ultra-secure interior

Image Source • Getty

ACCESS TUNNEL

INTERNAL BUILDING

BLAST DOORS
The blast doors are not on the main tunnel, but a side tunnel, which reduces the impact of the blast by 80 per cent. Each door weighs over 22 tons.

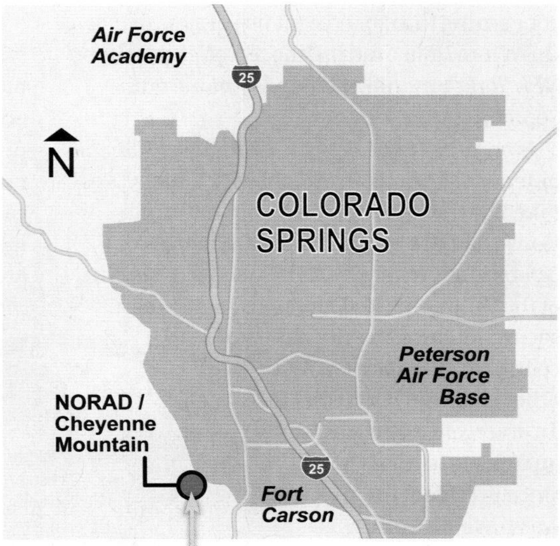

Air Force Academy
25

N

COLORADO SPRINGS

Peterson Air Force Base

NORAD / Cheyenne Mountain

Fort Carson
25

LOCATION
Being distant from either coast means missile flights would be longer, but the nearby Peterson Air Force base means it's close to a likely target.

Illustration • Adrian Mann

RESERVOIRS
Four reservoirs contain 6 million gallons of water to support those living in the complex.

ACCESS TUNNEL
The main access tunnel is open at both ends so any blast wave would pass straight through.

"NUCLEAR BUNKERS NEED TO PROVIDE AN ISOLATED LIVING ENVIRONMENT FOR SEVERAL MONTHS, PERHAPS UP TO A YEAR"

including national and regional war rooms, civil defence, communication facilities (including radio transmitting stations and telephone exchanges), water supplies, central and local government, fighter command and radar. A similar approach to providing protection for essential defence services was also taken in the United States, the construction of the Cheyenne Mountain Complex being just one example.

It would be interesting to know how these large bunkers in the United Kingdom and the United States would be used in the event of a nuclear threat, but needless to say, information is scant. Bearing in mind the furore following the recent discovery of a memory stick containing details of the route routinely taken by the queen from Buckingham Palace to Heathrow Airport, we can only imagine the level of secrecy surrounding such contingency plans. However, a few facts have come to light concerning the most recent use of a bunker at the White House during the terrorist attacks on New York, Virginia and Pennsylvania on 11 September 2001.

According to the reports, on realising the potential risk, Vice President Dick Cheney was taken by the Secret Service from his White House office to the Presidential Emergency Operations Center (PEOC) below the East Wing of the White House. This facility serves as a secure shelter and communications centre for the president and other essential personnel in an emergency. But this was an unusual situation since President Bush was travelling in

Florida, so the response was not typical. Instead, George W Bush took to the skies aboard Air Force One, escorted by three F-16 fighters, from where he managed the response to the attack in the 'Airborne Oval Office'.

In the UK and many other countries, nuclear bunkers were intended mainly to permit military and government operations to continue. Elsewhere, though, bunkers are sufficiently plentiful to provide a safe haven for a significant proportion of the population. Switzerland is the ultimate example, with laws in place since the 1960s ensuring that all new buildings are equipped with fallout shelters. As a result, 100 per cent of the population is now catered for, either in their own bunkers or in large-scale facilities designed for civilian protection. In other countries this level of preparedness might not be guaranteed, but this hasn't stopped people from taking precautions.

Some companies offering private nuclear shelters are currently reporting more orders per month than they received during the whole of 2016. And some of these are pretty lavish, providing a bit of luxury during those months of isolation. For between $1.5 and $4 million you can buy an apartment in an underground facility protected against the effects of a nuclear attack, with amenities including a cinema, indoor pool and spa, medical centre, bar, gym and library. Now surely that's the ultimate status symbol.

"WE CAN ONLY IMAGINE THE LEVEL OF SECRECY SURROUNDING CONTINGENCY PLANS"

SWISS FORT KNOX

Originally built as a Cold War nuclear bunker, a facility in the Swiss Alps is now home to a secure server farm designed to survive nuclear war. This is no official initiative, though, but the brainchild of two businessmen who offer their clients the ultimate in data security from risks as diverse as war, terrorism, environmental disasters and financial meltdown.

The so-called 'Swiss Fort Knox' is responsible for storing thousands of terabytes of data on behalf of 10,000 clients, including some of the world's largest corporations, such as Cisco Systems, UBS and Deutsche Bank. It also hosts data belonging to Planets, a project funded partially by the European Union with the aim of ensuring "long-term access to our digital, cultural and scientific assets".

LEFT Switzerland's Sonnenberg Tunnel was the world's largest civilian nuclear shelter, designed to protect 20,000 people

Image Source • Cooper

Cold War bunkers, like this one in York, had a most decidedly 'functional' look to them

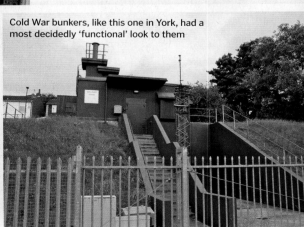

Image Source • Mike Peel

Image Source • U.S. Air Force photo/Master Sgt. Lance Cheung

Underground launch control centres still form a role in America's missile monitoring and launch capability

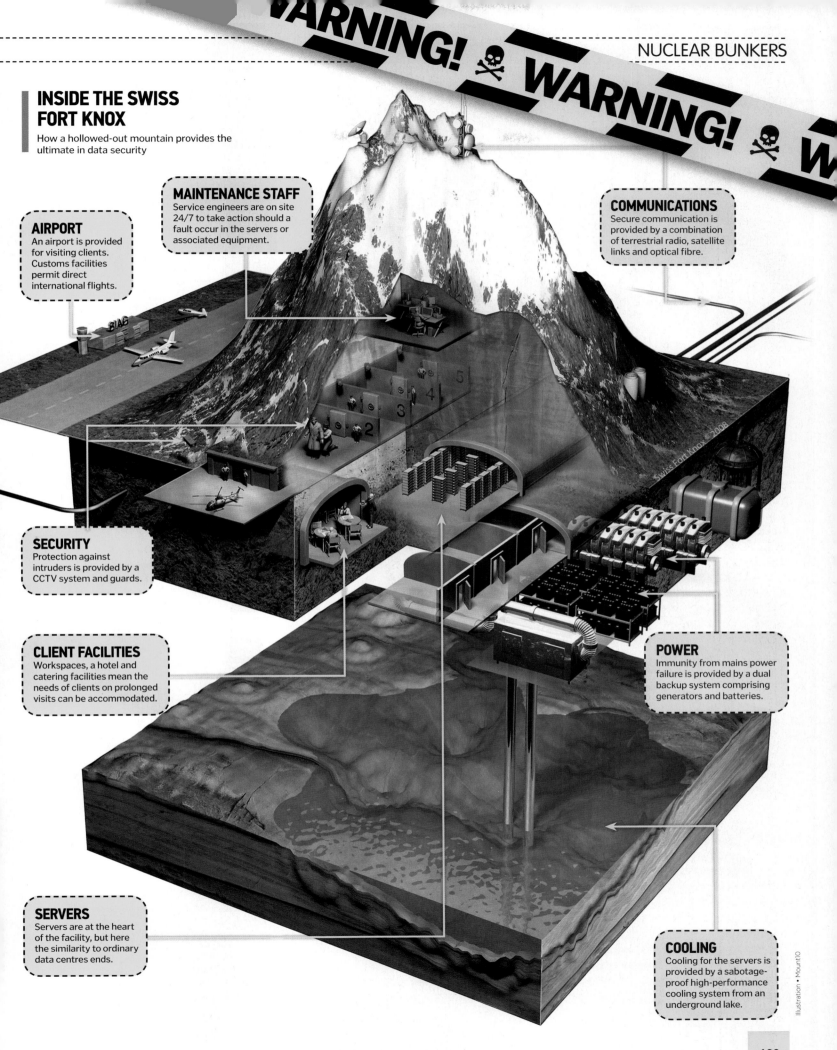

WARNING! ☠ WARNING! ☠ W

INSIDE THE SWISS FORT KNOX

How a hollowed-out mountain provides the ultimate in data security

AIRPORT
An airport is provided for visiting clients. Customs facilities permit direct international flights.

MAINTENANCE STAFF
Service engineers are on site 24/7 to take action should a fault occur in the servers or associated equipment.

COMMUNICATIONS
Secure communication is provided by a combination of terrestrial radio, satellite links and optical fibre.

SECURITY
Protection against intruders is provided by a CCTV system and guards.

CLIENT FACILITIES
Workspaces, a hotel and catering facilities mean the needs of clients on prolonged visits can be accommodated.

POWER
Immunity from mains power failure is provided by a dual backup system comprising generators and batteries.

SERVERS
Servers are at the heart of the facility, but here the similarity to ordinary data centres ends.

COOLING
Cooling for the servers is provided by a sabotage-proof high-performance cooling system from an underground lake.

Illustration • Mount10

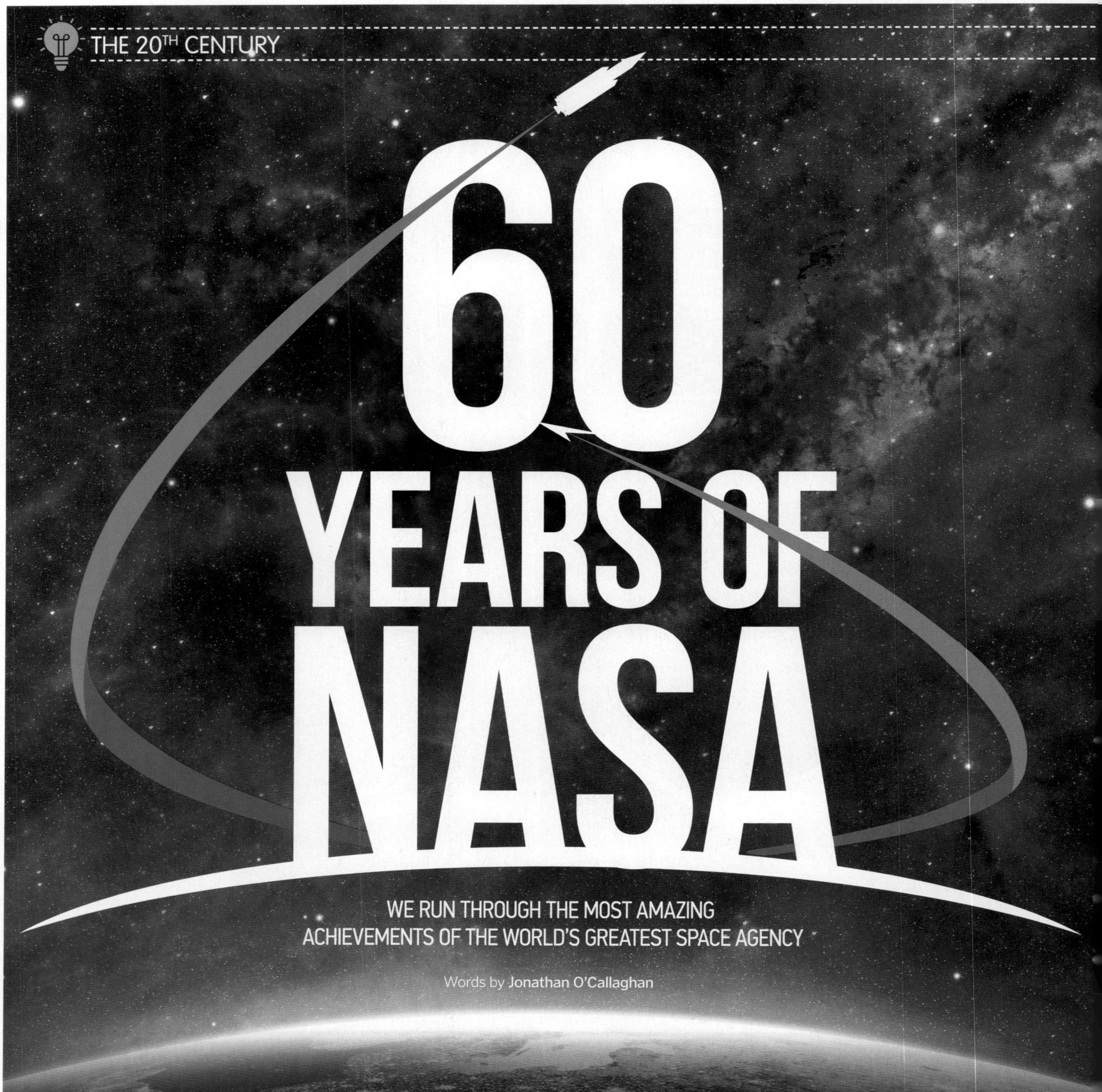

60 YEARS OF NASA

WE RUN THROUGH THE MOST AMAZING ACHIEVEMENTS OF THE WORLD'S GREATEST SPACE AGENCY

Words by Jonathan O'Callaghan

Image Source • Getty

When NASA first opened its doors on 1 October 1958, humans had never been to space. We had no idea what most of the other planets really looked like, we'd never even seen a comet or asteroid up close, and setting foot on another world was the stuff of dreams. Fast forward to today and our knowledge of space – thanks to NASA – is unlike anything we had thought possible.

The agency was born out of a battle to decide whether the American space agency should serve the military or civilians. Facing a growing threat from the Soviet Union, the US saw space as an opportunity to flex its considerable muscle and show off its envious technological prowess. However, numerous scientists argued in favour of NASA being used for strictly peaceful purposes, highlighting some of the grand questions about our universe that it could potentially answer and some of the fantastic locales that could be explored. Thankfully, they won out – NASA was set up with science at its core, and we're all the better for it.

NASA's primary goals were to expand human knowledge about space and develop vehicles that could take us to the stars. They tackled these challenges with aplomb, and today we've been treated to an endless cavalcade of science, from Moon landings to images of strange alien worlds.

The agency isn't going anywhere yet, and the future promises even more groundbreaking milestones. NASA's achievements of the past 64 years are incredible, but the best might be yet to come.

NASA

1 OCTOBER 1958

01 The National Aeronautics and Space Administration (NASA) opens its doors, becoming a civilian and scientific space agency for the United States. NASA was born from the ashes of the National Advisory Committee for Aeronautics (NACA), with some debate over whether the American space agency should be run for civilian or military purposes. After much conjecture from scientists and researchers, the former ultimately won out.

NASA began with 8,000 employees and an annual budget of $100 million. Today it boasts more than 17,000 and a budget of over $19 billion (£14.6 billion). And thanks to the early work of people fighting the corner for a peaceful space agency, NASA has grown to become the leading advocate of space science and exploration in the world. It has explored all the major planets, landed on the Moon, study Earth's climate, visited Pluto, and even sent spacecraft beyond the Solar System.

RIGHT **Pioneer was also designed to measure cosmic radiation**

11 OCTOBER 1958

02 NASA launches its first spacecraft, Pioneer 1, on top of a Thor-Able rocket. The spacecraft had an ambitious goal of reaching the Moon, but a programming error meant the probe fell back to Earth less than two days after launch.

3 MARCH 1959

03 Pioneer 4 launches, the first American spacecraft to pass by the Moon.

28 MAY 1959

04 Able and Baker become the first monkeys to survive a spaceflight.

5 MAY 1961

05 Alan Shepard becomes the first American in space (and the second human after Soviet Yuri Gagarin weeks prior) on the Freedom 7 spacecraft. During the 15-minute flight he reached an altitude of 187.5 kilometres before returning to Earth.

ABOVE **Alan Shepard pictured onboard the Freedom 7 spacecraft**

1950s | 1960s

---

20 FEBRUARY 1962

06 John Glenn becomes the first American to orbit the Earth.

10 JULY 1962

07 First communications satellite launched, Telstar 1.

23 MARCH 1965

08 First two US astronauts in space simultaneously, on Gemini 3.

15 JULY 1965

09 Mariner 4 returns the first close-up images of Mars.

2 JUNE 1966

10 First uncrewed US spacecraft, Surveyor 1, lands on the Moon.

21-27 DECEMBER 1968

11 The first humans orbit the Moon, on the Apollo 8 mission.

RIGHT **It's pretty hard to top the first ever landing on the Moon**

"NASA'S ACHIEVEMENTS OF THE PAST 60 YEARS ARE INCREDIBLE"

21 JULY 1969

12 Apollo 11 astronauts Neil Armstrong and Buzz Aldrin become the first humans to set foot on the surface of another world. This monumental event in human history ended the space race between the US and the Soviet Union, who had both set their sites on landing humans on the Moon.

Armstrong and Aldrin's lunar lander, called Eagle, touched down on the lunar surface in the afternoon on 20 July, although Armstrong would not take the first steps on the surface until the early hours of the morning of 21 July. Aldrin followed after, and the two conducted experiments, scooped up Moon rock, took pictures and left a plaque on the surface before returning home. It remains one of humanity's greatest ever achievements, let alone NASA's, watched by an audience in the hundreds of millions around the world.

Image Sources • NASA

11-17 APRIL 1970

13 Recovery of Apollo 13 after disaster strikes the mission.

26 JULY – 7 AUGUST 1971

14 Apollo 15, the first long-duration Moon mission with a rover.

14 NOVEMBER 1971

15 Mariner 9 becomes the first spacecraft to orbit another planet (Mars).

3 MARCH 1972 – 6 APRIL 1973

16 Pioneer 10 and 11 launch to visit Jupiter and Saturn.

7-19 DECEMBER 1972

17 Final crewed mission to the Moon, Apollo 17.

14 MAY 1973

18 Skylab, the first US space station, is launched.

15-24 JULY 1975

19 Joint mission with the Soviet Union, the Apollo-Soyuz Test Project.

Viking 1 and 2 were the first successful Mars landers and returned some amazing images

20 JULY 1976

20 The Viking 1 spacecraft becomes the first to ever land successfully on the surface of Mars. It remains operational for more than six years, searching for signs of life on the Red Planet and taking stunning images of the Martian surface.

1970s · 13 · 14 · 15 · 16 · 17 · 18 · 19 · 20 · 21 · 22 · 23 · **1980s** · 24 · 25 · 26 · 27 · 28 · 29 · 30

---

3 SEPTEMBER 1976

21 Viking 2 successfully lands on Mars.

20 AUGUST 1977

22 In the summer of 1965, NASA scientists discover that a rare alignment of the planets occurs once every 176 years, making possible a 'Grand Tour' of the four outer planets: Jupiter, Saturn, Uranus and Neptune. The culmination of this discovery was the Voyager mission, consisting of two spacecraft, Voyager 1 and 2, the former launched on 5 September 1977, the latter on 20 August 1977.

The two spacecraft returned the first ever images of the four giant planets and imaged dozens of their moons. We saw up close for the first time the rings of Saturn, the band of Jupiter, and much more. As the faster of the two, Voyager 1 also became the first human spacecraft ever to leave the Solar System. Both still continue to transmit as they make their way into interstellar space.

Voyager 1 and 2 opened up the outer Solar System like never before

4 DECEMBER 1978

23 The Pioneer Venus Orbiter enters orbit around Venus.

12 APRIL 1981

24 The Space Shuttle takes flight for the first time, with astronauts John Young and Robert Crippen onboard. The launch of Columbia heralded the world's first reusable space plane, with the main orbiter detaching from the external tank once in space and able to spend weeks in orbit before returning to land on a runway on Earth. This was the first US human spaceflight since 1975 and was lauded as one of the greatest aviation achievements in NASA's history.

The programme would go on to be wildly successful, if costly, with five orbiters completing 133 missions. Two flights would end in tragedy as Challenger exploded in 1986 after lift-off, killing its crew of seven, and Columbia broke apart on re-entry in 2003, also killing seven.

18-24 JUNE 1983

25 Sally Ride becomes the first US woman in space.

6-13 APRIL 1984

26 First satellite orbital repair mission, by Challenger.

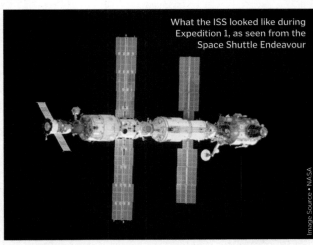

Image Source • NASA

24 JANUARY 1986 – 25 AUGUST 1989

27 The Voyager 2 spacecraft returns the first ever close-up images of Uranus and later Neptune, revealing these ice giants in all their glory. The probe captured amazing images of both planets and their moons and to this day remains the only spacecraft to ever visit these worlds.

24 JANUARY 1986

28 Voyager 2 performs the first and only Uranus flyby.

4 MAY 1989

29 Magellan spacecraft launches to map Venus' surface.

25 AUGUST 1989

30 First and only flyby of Neptune, by Voyager 2.

18 OCTOBER 1989

31 Galileo spacecraft launches on mission to orbit Jupiter.

Hubble has been one of the greatest space observatories ever launched

24 APRIL 1990

32 The Hubble Space Telescope is launched, the crowning achievement of NASA's astronomy programme and its most ambitious telescope at the time. Measuring 13.2 metres long and weighing nearly 11,000 kilograms, Hubble was lofted into orbit by Space Shuttle Discovery. However, shortly after launching a severe fault was found in its primary mirror, rendering all the telescope's images of the distant universe blurry. It wasn't until a complicated servicing mission in December 1993 was completed by the crew on Space Shuttle Endeavour that the telescope was up and running. It quickly began to completely redefine our view of the universe.

Hubble has snapped everything from glorious nebulae to distant galaxies, has helped us determine the age of the universe and even discovered new moons around Pluto. Today it is still going strong, with no end in sight.

"HUBBLE HAS SNAPPED EVERYTHING FROM GLORIOUS NEBULAE TO DISTANT GALAXIES"

1990s   **2000s**

29 OCTOBER 1991

33 Galileo performs the first ever asteroid flyby.

27 JUNE – 7 JULY 1995

34 Space Shuttle Atlantis docks to Russian space station Mir.

7 DECEMBER 1995

35 Galileo releases a probe into the atmosphere of Jupiter.

20 FEBRUARY 1997

36 Galileo finds evidence for a subsurface ocean on Jupiter's moon Europa.

4 JULY 1997

37 Mars Pathfinder becomes the first rover on Mars.

15 OCTOBER 1997

38 The Cassini probe launches, a bold mission to explore Saturn like never before. It would enter orbit in 2004, beginning a 13-year mission of multiple discoveries. It also deployed an ESA lander – Huygens – onto the moon Titan.

LEFT NASA stopped painting the Shuttle's external tank white after the second launch, as it was found that the paint increased the tank's weight by over 270kg

4 DECEMBER 1998

39 First US component of ISS launched, called Unity.

What the ISS looked like during Expedition 1, as seen from the Space Shuttle Endeavour

Image Source • NASA

2 NOVEMBER 2000

40 The first crew arrives at the fledgling International Space Station (ISS), consisting of just a few modules. Composed of NASA astronaut Bill Shepherd and Russian cosmonauts Sergei Krikalev and Yuri Gidzenko, the Expedition 1 mission began the continuous presence of humans in space that is still ongoing today.

The ISS was a monumental achievement for NASA, Russia and their other international partners, working together on a global mission like never before. The station's design was born out of a previous NASA project, called Space Station Freedom, but they realised it was too ambitious to undertake alone so they enlisted the help of others. Impressively, just decades after the Cold War, one of these partners happened to be America's former arch rival, a partnership in space that doesn't look like it's ending any time soon.

12 FEBRUARY 2001

41 NEAR Shoemaker becomes the first spacecraft ever to land on an asteroid.

28 MAY 2002

42 Mars Odyssey spacecraft finds signs of water ice deposits on Mars.

4–25 JANUARY 2004

43 Spirit and Opportunity rovers land on Mars.

1 JULY 2004

44 Cassini-Huygens enters orbit around Saturn.

4 JULY 2005

45 Deep Impact probe smashes crater on the comet Tempel 1.

15 JANUARY 2006

46 Stardust mission returns first dust from a comet.

9 MARCH 2006

47 Cassini finds geysers of water on Enceladus.

25 MAY 2008

48 Phoenix lander touches down on Mars.

Image Source • NASA

"NASA HOPES TO RETURN SAMPLES FROM THE SURFACE OF MARS"

8 SEPTEMBER 2016

60 OSIRIS-REx launches on a mission to asteroid Bennu.

15 SEPTEMBER 2017

61 Cassini mission ends with plunge into Saturn's atmosphere.

18 APRIL 2018

62 Transiting Exoplanet Survey Satellite (TESS) launches to find more exoplanets.

5 MAY 2018

63 InSight lander launches to Mars.

12 AUGUST 2018

64 The Parker Solar Probe launches on a mission to the Sun.

7 MARCH 2009

49 NASA's Kepler space telescope launches, the first space telescope designed to hunt for worlds outside the Solar System – exoplanets. The mission was a resounding success, discovering thousands of other planets and completely redefining our view of the galaxy.

The Kepler telescope has found the vast majority of known exoplanets to date

2000s 41 42 43 44 45 46 47 48 49 **2010s** 50 51 52 53 54 55 56 57 58 59 60 61 62 63 64

4 JANUARY 2010

50 Kepler detects its first planets beyond the Solar System.

11 FEBRUARY 2010

51 The Solar Dynamics Observatory launches to study the Sun.

18 MARCH 2011

52 MESSENGER spacecraft enters orbit around Mercury.

Curiosity landed in a region of Mars known as Gale Crater

Image Source • NASA

16 JULY 2011

53 Dawn spacecraft enters orbit around Vesta.

21 JULY 2011

54 Final flight of the Space Shuttle as Atlantis touches down.

6 AUGUST 2012

55 The Curiosity rover lands on Mars, NASA's most advanced rover ever sent to another world. Results from the rover, still going strong today, have suggested evidence for ancient water on Mars and the possibility it was once habitable.

25 AUGUST 2012

56 Voyager 1 reaches interstellar space.

6 MARCH 2015

57 Dawn orbits Ceres – the first spacecraft to orbit two celestial bodies.

5 JULY 2016

58 The solar-powered Juno spacecraft enters orbit around Jupiter.

14 JULY 2015

59 NASA's New Horizons spacecraft flies past Pluto, returning our first ever close up images of this distant world. It had launched into space on an Atlas V rocket on 19 January 2006, shooting into space at a speed of 58,536 kilometres per hour – the fastest spacecraft ever to leave Earth orbit. The journey to Pluto would take over nine years and cover a distance of 4.7 billion kilometres of space. New Horizons eventually flew past on 14 July 2015, sending back amazing images of the surface of Pluto and its largest moon Charon.

New Horizons is continuing on its way out of the Solar System today, and on 1 January 2019 it reached its next target, a small object in the distant Kuiper Belt far beyond Neptune called 2014 MU69, believed to be a remnant of the early Solar System.

New Horizons returned stunning images of Pluto to Earth

Image Source •

WHAT'S NEXT FOR NASA?

FIRST PRIVATE SPACECRAFT

On 20 December 2019, the first private spacecraft in NASA's Commercial Crew Program – built by SpaceX and Boeing – lifted off. These spacecraft have brought crewed launches back to US soil.

Image Source • NASA

SPACE LAUNCH SYSTEM

NASA launched its huge new Space Launch System (SLS) rocket for the first time on 16 November 2022. It will be used to take astronauts back to the Moon and maybe on to Mars.

Image Source • NASA

JAMES WEBB SPACE TELESCOPE

The much-delayed James Webb Space Telescope (JWST) launched on 25 December 2021. The successor to Hubble, it has already provided a glorious new view of the universe.

Image Source • SAIC; Northrop Grumman

Image Source • NASA

LUNAR SPACE STATION

NASA currently has tentative plans to launch a space station into lunar orbit in the 2020s called the Deep Space Gateway (DSG). The international collaboration will replace the ISS.

MISSIONS TO MARS

In the late 2020s NASA hopes to return samples from the surface of Mars with robotic probes. They still hope to send humans there in the 2030s.

Image Source • NASA; Pat Rawlings

SUBSCRIBE & SAVE UP TO 61%

Delivered direct to your door or straight to your device

Choose from over 80 magazines and make great savings off the store price!

Binders, books and back issues also available

Simply visit www.magazinesdirect.com

 No hidden costs   Shipping included in all prices   We deliver to over 100 countries   🔒 Secure online payment

┌ ┐
FUTURE **magazinesdirect**.com
└ ┘
Official Magazine Subscription Store